LEARNING TO
QUILT
THE TRADITIONAL WAY

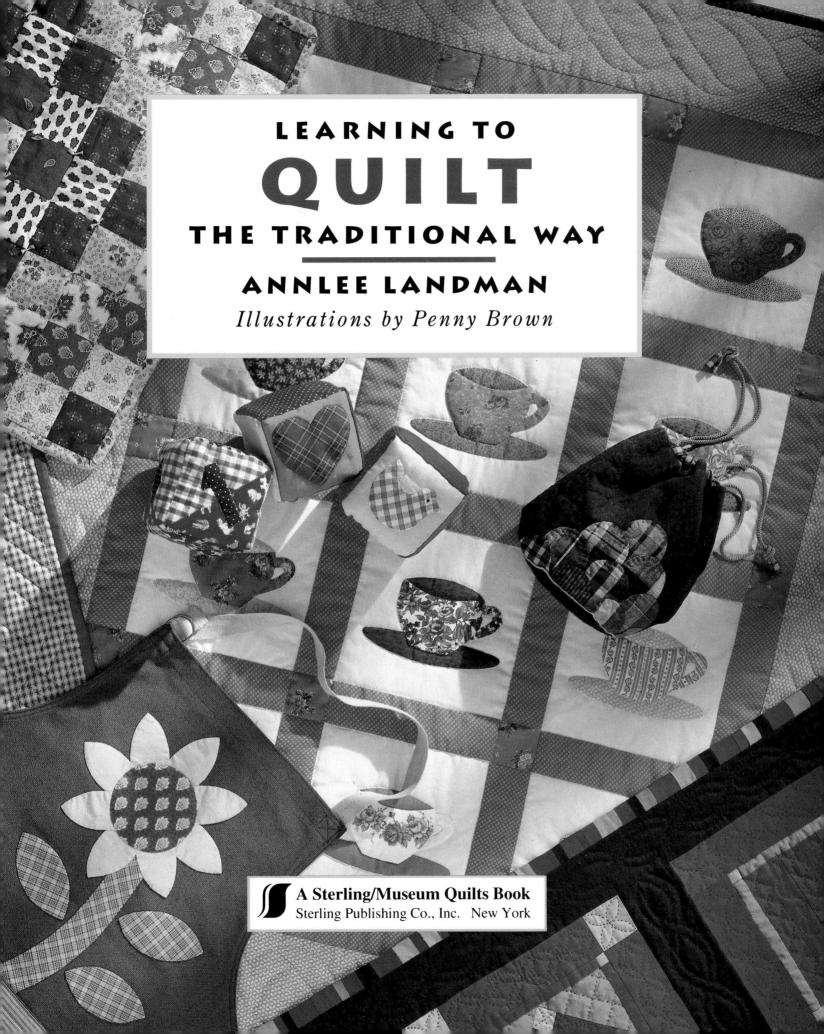

LEARNING TO QUILT
QUILT
THE TRADITIONAL WAY

ANNLEE LANDMAN

Illustrations by Penny Brown

A **Sterling/Museum Quilts Book**
Sterling Publishing Co., Inc. New York

A STERLING/MUSEUM QUILTS BOOK

Published by Sterling Publishing Company, Inc.
387 Park Avenue South, New York, NY 10016
And by Museum Quilts Publications
254-258 Goswell Road, London EC1V 7EB
Distributed in Canada by Sterling Publishing
·/o Canadian Manda Group, P.O. Box 920, Station U
Toronto, Ontario, Canada M8Z 5P9
Distributed in Australia by Capricorn Link (Australia) Pty Ltd.
P.O. Box 6651, Baulkham Hills, Business Centre, NSW 2153, Australia

The author has endeavored to ensure that all project instructions are accurate. However, due to variations in readers' individual skill and materials available, neither the author nor the publishers can accept responsibility for damages or losses resulting from the instructions herein. All instructions should be studied and clearly understood before beginning any project.

Editor: Ljiljana Ortolja-Baird
Design team: Judith Gordon and Edward Harbour
Title page photograph by Colin Mills

Library of Congress Cataloging-in-Publication Data

Landman, Annlee.
    Learning to quilt the traditional way / Annlee Landman ;
illustrations by Penny Brown.
        p.   cm.
    Includes index.
    ISBN 0-8069-0629-4   (Sterling Pub. Co.)
        1. Patchwork — Patterns.   2.   Quilting — Patterns   3. Appliqué -
Patterns.   4.   Quilted goods.   I. Title.
TT835.L328   1994
746.46 — d c 20   93 −40986
                                                                          CIP

2 4 6 8 10 9 7 5 3 1

Color origination by Dong-A Publishing and Printing Company, Ltd, Korea
Printed and bound in Korea

ISBN: 0-8069-0629-4

To Baba,
my beloved grandmother,
forever a source of inspiration,
courage and determination.

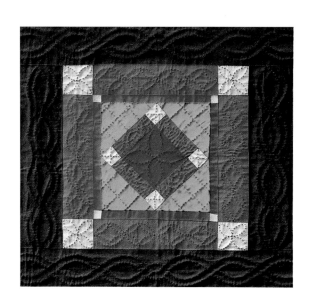

CONTENTS

THE PROJECTS

HOW TO GET STARTED

The projects have been designed for beginners who would like to learn the basic skills of quiltmaking while making something practical and attractive. They are all fairly small, so they will not be expensive to make and with the exception of the Basket and Teacup Quilts and the Amish Table Runner most can be completed in a day. Each project specifies a skill level. If you are drawn to the larger and more complicated projects, you could test your skills by making a single block.

EQUIPMENT

COLORED PENCILS
Use hard lead and colored pencils for marking fabrics - blue on light colored fabric and yellow or white pencils to mark dark fabrics.

DRAFTING TRIANGLE
An essential tool for squaring off the raw edges of your fabric and for strip cutting. Do not use a triangle smaller than 6 inches.

LONG RULER
Use with a drafting triangle for straightening edges and drawing lines for strip cutting. You may want to buy a clear plastic quilter's ruler which is marked with horizontal and vertical grid lines - a help when strip cutting and marking seam allowances.

NEEDLES
Use SHARPS for hand piecing and appliqué, BETWEENS for quilting, and DARNING or MILLINERS needles for basting. The needle size is denoted by number - the higher the number, the finer the needle.

PINS
Fine, stainless steel dressmaker's pins are best. Throw away rusty, bent or burred pins as they can damage your fabric. For assembling the three quilt layers, use extra long, glass-head quilting pins. You can also use safety pins to pin-baste the layers together.

SEAM RIPPER
A useful tool for unpicking machine-sewn stitches.

SCISSORS
Dressmaker's shears are very sharp and should only be used for cutting fabric. They usually have a bent handle to make cutting easier. Use kitchen scissors or a utility knife for cutting paper or templates.

TEMPLATE MATERIAL
Cardboard and clear template plastic are both suitable for making reusable templates

THIMBLE
This item is essential for hand quilting to help push your needle through the quilt layers. It should be metal with a flat top and fit snugly on the middle finger of your sewing hand.

THREAD
For machine and hand sewing, use standard cotton thread. Choose a color that matches the darkest fabric you are sewing. When sewing together different colored fabrics use a neutral gray or ecru thread. For quilting, use a 100% cotton quilting thread. Pearl cotton is suitable for Sashiko.

TRACING PAPER
If not using template plastic, trace the template shape onto tracing paper then glue it onto a piece of firm cardboard. Cut out the shape to make a reusable template.

OTHER EQUIPMENT

SEWING MACHINE

A sewing machine is not absolutely essential. Although all the projects in this book can be hand pieced, machine piecing is much faster.

IRON

An essential item for setting seams and aligning rows.

QUILTING HOOP

A hoop keeps the three layers of the quilt sandwich taut and smooth while hand quilting. It is a portable alternative to a quilting frame and helps maintain an even tension across your fabric, which gives your quilting stitch greater definition. Provided your work is well basted, quilting hoops are not essential for small projects.

ALL ABOUT FABRIC

Walk into any fabric shop and you are sure to be surprised by the variety available. Since fabric is the most important element in any quilt or quilted project, what you choose requires careful consideration.

To begin with, restrict your selection to 100% cotton, dress weight fabric. It is easy to cut, sew and mark. It is durable, washes well and stands up to the heat of an iron allowing it to hold a crease. It is usually manufactured with a medium weave that will not fray easily and will not allow the batting to seep through.

When you look at a quilt pattern on paper it is flat and rather lifeless. It is the fabric, its color, value, scale and pattern that will bring a project to life. By changing the fabric placement or by using fabrics of different value and density

the same quilt design will appear completely different. For most quiltmakers the most difficult decision is choosing a color scheme. Color preference is strictly an individual issue; there is no right or wrong and there are no strict rules to follow. It is important that you select colors that you will enjoy working and living with. Here are some pointers you should keep in mind:

✄ Aim for a variety of patterns using a combination of large and small scale prints.

✄ Combine printed fabrics with solids or plain fabrics to give relief to an otherwise busy quilt.

✄ If you are having trouble narrowing down your color options, try building your theme around a particular color in the room where the quilt may live. Pick out the dominant solid colors and a few small scale prints that complement the selection.

✄ Try to avoid over coordinating your fabrics. This will result in a dull and contrived looking quilt. Monochromatic projects can be successful, but must have lots of contrast between the lightest and darkest shade.

✄ Contrast in color and in pattern density will add richness and variety. Mix close, compact designs with large, open designs. If your pattern pieces are quite small, widely spaced prints will be wasted.

✄ Combine fabrics of different color value, by using light, medium and dark colors to create depth and texture. Darker and richer shades of color can be used to add definition to lighter or brighter colors, helping them to stand out.

 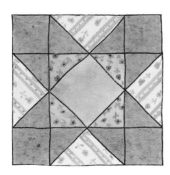  

✄ Use stripes, plaids and other geometric prints to add motion and visual excitement. Some directional fabrics, if not cut in a special way, may be unsettling in the overall quilt design.

✄ Combine small scale florals with ginghams, checks and pin dots in warm colors to achieve a traditional country look.

✄ If you have found a fabric that you want to use, but it is too dominant, or you need a lighter value, try turning it over. Sometimes the wrong side will provide the perfect solution.

✄ Select a suitable background fabric which can carry the overall design. Muslin, a solid, a small overall print, or a broken print which will appear solid from a distance are good choices.

✄ Do not to mix materials of varying weights as this can cause uneven wear and stress on the seams. You may not know whether the fabric is 100% cotton or a polyester cotton blend, so you will need to take special care, as laundering and ironing temperatures may differ. This is especially important if you are planning to use scrap fabrics.

✄ If you are tempted to recycle old clothes make sure the fabric is not worn.

✄ Chintz, polished cotton and other lightweight furnishing fabrics are attractive alternatives to dress fabrics, but they present several problems. They tend to be very tightly woven and are not suitable for hand sewing. Pins and stitching may also leave permanent holes, so try a test seam before incorporating it in your project. As the distinctive glazed finish tends to dull with washing, these fabrics are probably best saved for wall hangings or other items that will not require laundering.

✄ Since it is difficult to see the finished quilt at this early stage in the quiltmaking process, you must be content to use trial and error in choosing your fabrics. One way to help you visualize the finished result is to trace the outline of the block several times, then use colored pencils to experiment with different color schemes.

Another option is to pin or sew a single block as a trial, before you cut ALL the pieces. However, keep in mind that although you may like the look of a single block on its own, this unit when repeated will take on a different look. New patterns, designs and focal points are likely to emerge.

Once your selections have been made, lay your swatches out or stack the bolts of cloth on a table, take two steps back and squint. This simple exercise will help you test for color balance. If you are not completely happy with the combination, do not hesitate to make changes.

The color photographs of the finished projects are merely suggestions of how to interpret the design. Experiment with fabric. A bold fabric which on its own seems loud, next to another could provide the vital contrast to make your project sparkle.

BACKING FABRIC

Fabric for the quilt backing should be of the same weight and quality as the quilt top. Avoid using bedsheets as backing, unless they are 100% cotton. Although the size may be right, most percale bed linen has too high a thread count and is too tightly woven to be quilted through.

If you are planning to self-bind the quilt, by bringing the excess backing fabric to the front, choose a fabric that coordinates with the quilt top and will not show through to the front. Some dark prints will give a cast to a predominantly light quilt top.

A solid or plain backing fabric will highlight the overall quilting pattern. If however, you would rather conceal uneven quilting stitches, choose a printed fabric.

PREPARING YOUR FABRIC

For best results most experts advise pre-washing fabrics. This will allow the expected 2-3% shrinkage to occur before your quilt is pieced. Washing softens the fabric by removing the sizing and chemicals used in the manufacturing process.

TO PRE-WASH YOUR FABRICS

1. Unfold to a single thickness and sort into lights and darks.

2. Make several short snips along the length of the selvage to allow even shrinkage.

3. Wash in the washing machine using a small amount of mild liquid soap on a warm wash cycle. Double rinse.

4. As you remove your wet fabric from the machine, rub a corner of each length on a piece of white fabric. If there is any sign of dye on the white fabric your fabric is not colorfast and you will need to set the dye.

5. Hang the fabric out to dry, or tumble dry on a low temperature setting. Remove the fabric while still damp and press.

✄ While most fabrics today are colorfast, some of the darker, more vivid colors tend to bleed. Do NOT mix washed and unwashed yardage as you will have uneven shrinkage which could distort your project. In addition, you might inadvertently include a fabric which is not colorfast and ruin your project.

Pre-washing is a personal choice. Many quilters prefer to work with crisp, new cloth as it is has not been softened and it can be sewn more accurately. If you would rather wash the project after it has been made up to give it a wrinkled, antique appearance, you take the risk that your fabrics may bleed.

If you do not intend to pre-wash, you should at least test your fabric for colorfastness BEFORE you begin piecing.

TESTING YOUR FABRIC IF YOU CHOOSE NOT TO PRE-WASH

1. Fill a clear jar with warm water and a drop of mild liquid soap.

2. Cut a 2 inch square of each fabric to be tested. Place one swatch in the water. Let the fabric soak.

3. Check to see if the water has discolored. If it remains clear, continue with the next swatch, one at a time.

4. If the water discolors you will need to set the dye in a solution of one part clear white vinegar to three parts cold water. Let the fabric soak, then rinse it until the water runs clear.

5. To double check that the dye has set, wash it again and while still wet, rub against a piece of white fabric. Rinse again.

6. If after treating with the vinegar solution you still cannot set the dye, choose a substitute fabric.

GETTING TO KNOW YOUR QUILT

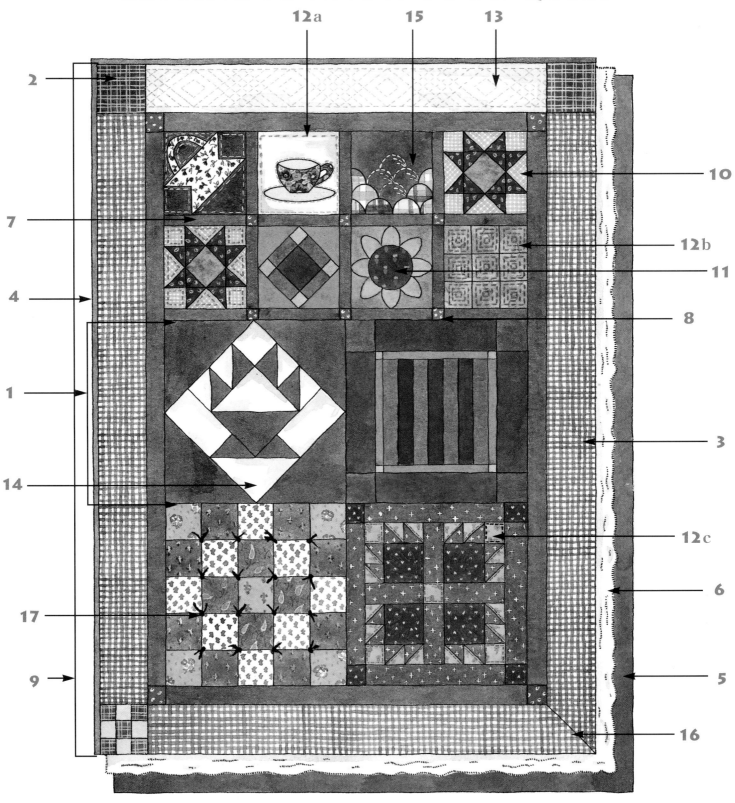

1. **BLOCK**
2. **CORNER BLOCK**
3. **BORDER**
4. **BINDING**
5. **BACKING**
6. **BATTING**
7. **SASHING**
8. **POST**
9. **QUILT TOP**
10. **PIECED BLOCK**

11. **APPLIQUÉ**
12. **QUILTING**
    (a) **OUTLINE QUILTING**
    (b) **ECHO QUILTING**
    (c) **IN-THE-DITCH QUILTING**
13. **QUILTING PATTERN**
14. **ON-POINT SETTING**
15. **SASHIKO**
16. **MITER**
17. **TYING OR TUFTING**

1. BLOCK: a single unit of a quilt, either pieced or appliquéd, which is repeated to make up the quilt top.

2. CORNER BLOCK: a plain or pieced square unit at each corner of a border. It adds further design interest and eliminates the need for a mitered border.

3. BORDER: a band of fabric of any width which can be plain or pieced, used to frame the interior section of a quilt. When multiple borders are used, they are called inside and outside borders. Borders are an optional design element in a quilt and provide a large area to exhibit your quilting ability. They can be used to enlarge a quilt without having to piece additional blocks.

4. BINDING: the enclosing and finishing of raw edges of a quilt either by self-binding or separate binding.

5. BACKING: the fabric that makes up the bottom layer of a quilt.

6. BATTING: the fluffy middle layer of a quilt that provides thickness (or loft) and warmth. It is available in a variety of fibers, including cotton, polyester, polyester-cotton blend, wool and silk. Polyester is recommended for beginners as it is easier to quilt, washes well, requires less quilting and gives a thicker, more dimensional appearance. Batting can be purchased by the yard or pre-packaged to standard bed sizes.

7. SASHING: plain or pieced strips used to separate quilt blocks. Also a method of enlarging a quilt without having to piece additional blocks. Sometimes known as lattice, these strips frame the individual blocks and can be used to unify the design.

8. POST: fabric squares that join and separate sashing strips at the intersection of each block.

9. QUILT TOP: the pieced, appliquéd or wholecloth fabric that makes up the decorative top layer of a quilt.

10. PIECED BLOCK: a square unit of a patchwork quilt made up of fabric pieces cut to a particular shape and sewn together to create a pattern.

11. APPLIQUÉ: sewing cut fabric shapes onto a background fabric.

12. QUILTING: the stitches made either by hand or machine that keep the three layers of a quilt together.

   (a) OUTLINE QUILTING: a row of quilting stitches that run parallel to the seam lines. This method of quilting requires no marking on the quilt top and is traditionally worked 1/4 inch away from the seam line.

   (b) ECHO QUILTING: a repetitive series of quilting lines stitched in equally spaced rows that echo the shape and pattern of a block design.

   (c) IN-THE-DITCH QUILTING: quilting stitches that seem to sink into the seam line and are stitched in a matching color thread as close as possible to the seam. It adds texture to a quilt without distracting from the piecing design.

13. QUILTING PATTERN: a decorative design that is achieved by the careful stitching of many tiny running stitches.

14. ON-POINT SETTING: a quilt block standing on its point so that its diagonal is oriented in a vertical direction.

15. SASHIKO: a traditional form of Japanese quilting which has been adapted by western quilters. This type of work is characterised by long (five to six stitches per inch) and even stitches in geometric patterns, using heavy white thread against an indigo background.

16. MITER: a method of finishing a corner by joining vertical and horizontal strips of fabric at a 45 degree angle.

17. TYING or TUFTING: an alternative method of securing the three quilt layers. Instead of using a quilting stitch, yarn or thread is tied through the quilt at regular intervals.

BASIC TECHNIQUES

CUTTING

Each project in this book includes detailed cutting instructions for either the template or strip cutting method. When templates are not included, measurements for pattern pieces are given. The fabric requirements listed under **MATERIALS** assume that you are careful and economical about laying out and cutting your pieces. If you are unsure of your cutting skills, buy slightly more yardage. Leftover fabric, either strips or pieces, can always be used in another project.

✂ **Yardage requirements are based on standard fabric widths of 44-45 inches.**

Accuracy in cutting your fabric is critical to successful piecing. Whether you are cutting your pieces from strips or from templates, they must be exactly the right size for your block to fit together.

Before cutting your fabric, it is important to familiarize yourself with some key words - selvage, bias, lengthwise grain and crosswise grain.

Selvages are the densely woven finished edges of fabric which should be trimmed off before sewing.

Grain is the direction of the threads in a fabric. **Crosswise grain** runs at right angles to the selvages and is slightly stretchy. **Lengthwise grain** runs parallel to the selvages and has little stretch. Grain lines are marked on your template with an arrow.

Bias runs at a 45 degree angle to the selvages and has the maximum stretch.

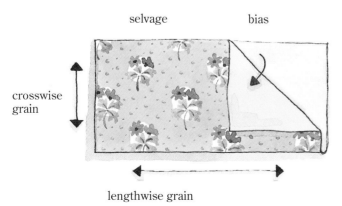

PREPARING YOUR FABRIC FOR CUTTING

1. Find the grain line by folding the fabric in half, selvage to selvage, with right sides facing. Hold the selvages together while leaving the fold to hang freely. Shift one side of the fabric until the fold hangs straight and smooth. The foldline is the straight, lengthwise grain. Press the fold flat.

2. Lay the fabric on a flat surface. Straighten the uneven raw edges of the fabric by lining up the bottom edge of a drafting triangle along the fold and place a ruler on the raw edge. Draw a pencil line along the length of the ruler and trim away the raw edge. Your fabric is now squared off and ready for cutting.

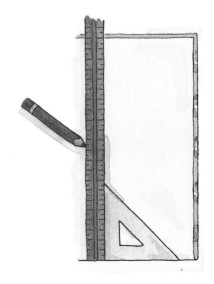

CUTTING FABRIC FROM STRIPS

When marking strips, move your ruler to the required width along the fold of the fabric. The ruler must be parallel to the straight squared off edge. To ensure your ruler is perfectly straight, line it up with the base of a drafting triangle which has been squared up with the folded edge of the fabric. Draw a pencil line against the edge of the ruler to mark the required width.

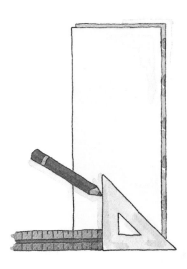

Use pins between marked lines to keep the two layers together while you carefully cut the strip.

Before cutting the strips, trim off the selvages. To cut squares and rectangles from the strips, measure along the length from the trimmed selvage end, mark a straight line and cut.

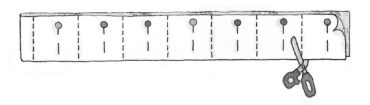

As a general rule, if using the same fabric for both the block and borders, it is best to cut the longest pieces first. Then cut the smaller pieces from the remaining yardage.

To cut triangles, first cut squares then cut them in half across the diagonal.

ROTARY CUTTING

Rotary cutting is a form of strip cutting. Although not a traditional method, the speed and accuracy of this revolutionary tool has made it a popular choice among quilt makers.

The cutter is shaped rather like a pizza-cutter with a replaceable razor-sharp blade, capable of cutting through up to eight layers of fabric. A rotary cutter must be used with a special self-healing mat which can be bought at most art supply shops. Mats come in various sizes and are marked with imperial or metric grids. You will also need a quilter's ruler - a transparent plastic ruler of various widths and marked with a horizontal and vertical grid.

If you are using a rotary cutter for the first time it is well worth spending time practicing with your new tools before embarking on a project.

1. Place your mat on a hard, flat surface.

2. Fold your fabric, selvage to selvage and press the fold flat. Refold to the selvage to make four layers and press again. Do not use your iron on your cutting mat, otherwise you will damage both iron and mat.

3. Carefully place your folded fabric on the mat with the raw edges to the right and left.

4. Place your ruler on the fabric at right angles to the fold, with the right long edge of the ruler near the right-hand raw edge of the fabric, but not covering it. Left-handed people will reverse this placement.

5. With your hand firmly on the ruler, place the cutter at the folded edge of the fabric. Keep the blade vertical and against the ruler. If the blade is turned out your cut edge will not be straight. With one firm motion roll the cutter along the ruler away from you. Keep the ruler steady and finish your cut beyond the selvages. Do not make short jerky movements.

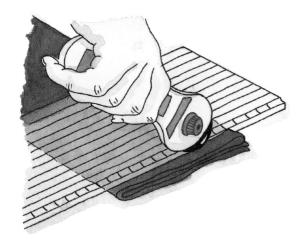

If **hand piecing**, follow the broken line for tracing your reusable template. This line will be your sewing line. Cut out each shape adding a 1/4 inch seam allowance.

6. Unfold the strip and check whether it is straight. If there is a kink or bend in the fabric, refold your fabric carefully and recut.

A rotary cutter is a very sharp tool and there are a few safety tips, worth remembering:

1. always cut away from yourself.

2. do not cut from side to side as it too difficult to control the blade pressure adequately.

3. when finished always cover the blade with a guard and keep it well away from children.

USING TEMPLATES FOR CUTTING

A template is a master pattern piece made of plastic or stiff cardboard around which to trace the shape onto fabric.

The template you cut depends on whether you will be machine or hand piecing your quilt. In this book, templates for machine piecing and appliqué are denoted by a solid line, hand piecing by a broken line.

If **machine piecing**, trace around the solid line to make your templates. This includes 1/4 inch seam allowance and enables you to mark the pieces adjacent to one another to give you the most efficient use of your fabric.

For either method place the template face down on the wrong side of the fabric. Start at least 1/2 inch away from the trimmed selvage. Align the arrow marked on the template along the lengthwise grain of the fabric. This eliminates the possibility of distortion when piecing and will give the finished block more stability because the straight grain will run along the outside edges of the block.

Carefully trace the shapes onto the fabric using a sharp pencil. Use light colored pencils on dark fabric and medium colored pencils on light fabrics. Never use a ball-point pen or a marking pen.

CUTTING FOR APPLIQUÉ

Position the template right side up on the right side of the fabric. Use a pencil or white dressmaker's chalk to mark around the template. Leave enough space between the pieces to cut a 1/4 inch seam allowance around each shape. The tracing lines are your fold-under and stitching lines.

SEWING THE PIECES

Before starting to sew, examine the block you will be piecing to determine the sewing sequence. Usually the smallest pieces are sewn together first and then joined to make larger and larger units until the block is complete. Other quilt blocks

start from a central unit and are built up by progressively adding borders.

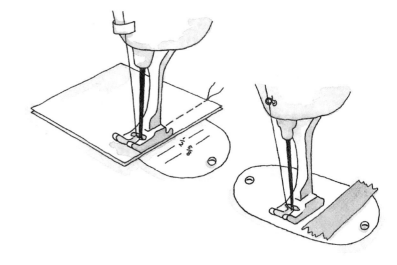

When sewing identical units, sew the pieces together assembly line fashion, feeding the pieces under the presser foot without cutting the thread. Provided your stitch length is small enough, there is no need to backstitch at the beginning and end of each pair of units. This method of sewing is also referred to as chain piecing. Snip the units apart once they have been sewn and press seam allowances towards the darker fabric before crossing them with another seam.

MACHINE PIECING

To machine piece, set the stitch length at 10-12 stitches per inch. Thread the machine with either a neutral color thread or a color that blends with the fabrics you have chosen. With right sides facing and edges matching, pin the pieces together with the pins at right angles to the seam line. Sew the pieces together from edge to edge. For machine piecing, there are no marked lines to guide your stitching. Instead, the seam line is measured exactly $1/4$ inch away from the cut edge of the fabric.

Sew a test seam on some scrap fabric using the outside edge of the presser foot as a guide. Measure the distance between the stitching line and the cut edge of the fabric. If this is exactly $1/4$ inch use the presser foot as your sewing guide. If not, mark the throat plate by carefully measuring $1/4$ inch to the right of the needle. Place several layers of masking tape at the point you have identified.

Successful patchwork with precise seam alignment depends on being able to sew $1/4$ inch seam accurately and consistently. The following hints will help you achieve perfect piecing:

1. When joining rows, press seams in opposite directions so that the pressed seams lock as they are sewn together. Use pins to keep the seam allowances from flipping over.

2. When piecing triangles, seam allowances intersect to give a reference point for matching seams. Use a positioning pin placed through the center of the X. Sew the seam straight through the center of the X to achieve a perfect point. If your seam allowance is not accurate, the points of the sewn triangles will either be chopped off or they will not meet the seam line.

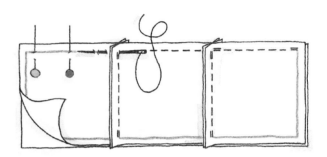

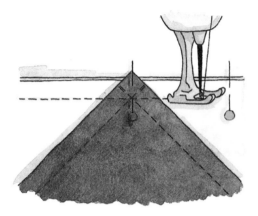

HAND PIECING

For hand piecing strip-cut fabric, you will need to mark each piece with a 1/4 inch seam allowance. Use a pencil and ruler to ensure that this is done accurately, as this will be your sewing line. If you have used the template method the sewing line will already be marked.

Pin the pieces together matching corners and marked sewing lines. Thread a needle with a single strand of matching color thread. Knot the end. Starting with a backstitch, sew from seam line to seam line rather than from raw edge to raw edge, leaving seam allowances open. Use a small, even running stitch, rocking your needle back and forth through the work, loading three to five stitches on the needle at a time before pulling it through. Turn your work over periodically to check that your stitches are staying on the pencil line. Finish your seam with another backstitch.

When you cross the seam allowances of smaller units, stitch through them without sewing them down. To do this, make a backstitch just before you cross over to the next piece. Then, pass the needle through the seam allowance and make another backstitch immediately after the seam allowance before continuing with the seam.

HOW TO APPLIQUÉ

Several projects in this book feature appliqué - a technique of layering or applying one piece of fabric onto another, which is then stitched down with a blind hem stitch. Ideally, appliqué should have smooth curves, crisp points and corners with barely visible stitching.

There are three appliqué methods. For each method, fabric pieces are marked from finished size templates on the right side of the fabric to give an accurate sewing line. To each shape add a scant 1/4 inch all around to allow for turning under.

METHOD 1

Pin appliqué patches in position on the background fabric. Use the tip of your needle to turn under short sections of the seam allowance along the pencil line as you go. Use your thumb and forefinger to finger press the seam allowance under. Stitch in place just inside the pencil line on the fold.

METHOD 2

Fold and baste under the seam allowance to the wrong side, just inside the pencil line on the fold. You may find it helpful to use the edge of the template as a guide, over which to press the seam allowance before basting.

METHOD 3

Appliqué using an iron-on interfacing. This method adds stability to lightweight fabrics. Use the same finished size template to cut out the appliqué shape from the interfacing. Do NOT add any seam allowance when cutting. Press the interfacing to the wrong side of the cut fabric piece inside the pencil line. Fold the fabric seam allowance over the edge of the interfacing to the wrong side and stitch down.

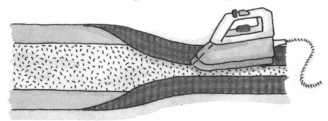

Whatever method you use for appliqué, you may need to clip into the seam allowance to make it easier to manipulate the seam allowance under. Be very careful when making these cuts not to snip beyond the pencil line.

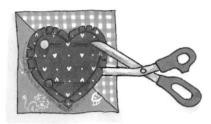

For all methods, first baste or pin the appliqué shape in position on the prepared background fabric which has either been folded or basted with placement guidelines. Use a **Sharps** needle with a single strand of matching color thread about 20 inches long. Bring the needle up through the background fabric, catching a few threads of the folded edge of the appliqué. Insert the needle back down through the background fabric, a fraction above the spot where it came up, and move the needle about 1/8 inch away for the next stitch. Keep the stitches reasonably snug, but not so tight that they pucker. They should show on the front as a tiny spot of thread, with a slightly longer stitch showing on the back. At the end

of a thread, take a backstitch and knot the thread from the back. Remove the basting stitches after the appliqué pieces have been sewn.

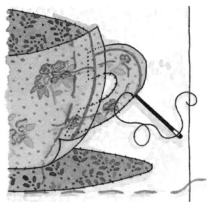

In more complicated appliqué designs where pieces will be overlapped or partially covered by others, stitch the underneath piece to the background fabric first. In general, it is best to work from background to foreground, making sure not to turn under edges that will be covered by another appliqué piece.

PRESSING AND IRONING

Correct and frequent pressing is an integral part of successful patchwork. Keep your iron and ironing board set up close to your work area. Your iron should be kept smooth and clean, and in good working order. If it has a tendency to spit or leak water, it may damage your work.

There is an important distinction between ironing and pressing. When ironing, you push or slide the iron, smoothing wrinkles and puckers as you go. This motion is correct for your quilt backing, which may have only a few long seams, if any. Quilt blocks on the other hand, have short, narrow seams which have been pressed to one side. The up-and-down motion of pressing is necessary to prevent distortion by stretching a seam out of shape.

Use a steam or ordinary iron with the temperature set for cotton. If you prefer to use a dry iron, lightly spray your block before pressing. This helps to achieve flat, smooth blocks with sharp seams.

Always PRESS the block first on the wrong side, to set the seams in the correct position, and then on the right side. When pressing on the right side, use a cloth to protect the surface from glazing.

Always press a seam towards the darker fabric to avoid shadowing through to the front of the quilt. If this cannot be avoided, trim the darker seam allowance narrower than the light one. Never press the seams open.

Press the seams of adjacent rows in opposite directions. This is particularly important because when the rows are pinned right sides together to be joined, the pressed seams will lock into place.

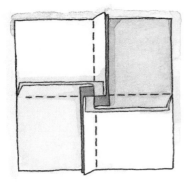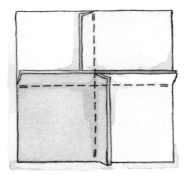

If you intend to quilt close to a seam line, try to press the seams to the opposite side. Alternatively, adjust your quilting plans, because it is very difficult to hand quilt through seam allowances.

JOINING THE BLOCKS TOGETHER

Once all the blocks have been pieced or appliquéd, they must be joined to make the quilt top. Lay the blocks out in a pleasing arrangement, pinning and labeling them so that you can sew them together in sequence according to your design. When joining blocks into rows, and when joining rows of blocks together, take special care to match the seams exactly.

This is easy to achieve provided you press the seam allowances in opposite directions for alternate rows. If any of the seams do not match neatly, you may need to ease or stretch the fabric to fit.

FINISHING

Once you have completed your quilt top, there are several steps you need to follow before it can be quilted and bound.

1. PRESSING THE QUILT TOP

Press your finished quilt top on the wrong side first to set the seams. Make sure all the seams lie flat. Inspect the back carefully and trim any loose threads and unraveled edges which may show through to the front of the quilt. Turn the quilt over and press again using a pressing cloth. This will be the last time your quilt top will be pressed, so be thorough. DO NOT iron the quilt after the batting has been attached, as the heat and weight of the iron will flatten it.

2. MARKING YOUR QUILTING PATTERN

In planning and marking your quilting pattern, it is important to keep in mind the requirements of the batting you intend to use. If you are using polyester batting, quilting lines may be as far apart as 6-8 inches. Traditional cotton batting requires much closer quilting - every 2 inches - to prevent the batting from shifting and becoming lumpy.

Quilting patterns should be marked on the right side of the quilt top before the layers are basted together. To prevent the top from moving while marking, the top should be taped down to a hard, flat surface.

The procedure for marking quilting templates is the same as for marking fabric for cutting. First, test your marking tools on a piece of scrap fabric to ensure that they will not permanently mark the fabric, nor disappear before the quilting is finished.

If your fabric is of a light color, you may be able to place the pattern under the quilt top and trace the quilting design directly onto the fabric with a clean, continuous line. If necessary, trace or photocopy the design from the book and then darken the lines with a permanent marking pen to make it easier to see the design through the fabric.

If your fabric is too dark to trace the pattern, use a sheet of dressmaker's carbon (placing the carbon face down on the fabric) between the quilting pattern and the quilt top. Then, using a tracing wheel, carefully follow the lines of the quilting design to transfer the outline to the fabric underneath.

Another attractive style of quilting which does not require marking and can easily be done by eye is **Echo Quilting**. This method follows the contour of a shape with a series of concentric outlines.

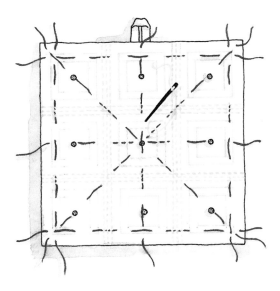

Most of the hand and machine quilting in this book requires no marking because it follows the seams of the patchwork. **Outline Quilting** is worked 1/4 inch away from the seam line, either by eye or along the edge of special 1/4 inch wide masking tape used as a stitching guide. If you prefer to follow a line, lightly mark the straight lines with a pencil and ruler.

In-the-Ditch Quilting is also called sink-stitching, because with this method quilting stitches are worked directly along the seam line, just to the side opposite the pressed seam allowances. The quilting stitches are barely visible and disappear into the seams. It is an effective way to get depth without detracting from the piecing.

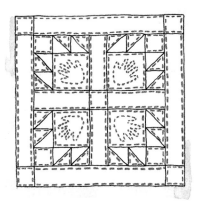

3. BACKING

Select backing fabric of similar quality and weight as in the quilt top. 100% cotton is best and easiest for quilting. Plain or printed fabric is suitable, but you should be certain that neither the color nor pattern shows through the batting to the quilt top. If it is visible, change to a lighter colored backing fabric.

The quilt backing should be cut at least 2 inches larger than the quilt top on all sides to allow for shrinkage during quilting. If you plan to self-bind, that is, to bring the backing forward to make the binding for your quilt, add another inch all around.

If the quilt or project is wider than 40 inches you will need to piece two widths of backing fabric. Seams may run either vertically or horizontally across the back of the quilt, depending on your preference and the most economical use of the fabric.

Trim off the selvages before seaming the pieces of fabric, using a 1/4 inch seam allowance. Press the seams to one side, never open, as with time and wear the batting may seep through the stitch holes.

Tape the backing onto a hard, flat surface before adding the batting.

4. BATTING

Batting is available in several different weights with varying fiber content. Your choice of batting should depend on the way in which you plan to use your quilt and the amount of loft or thickness you prefer. Batting is sold prepackaged for standard bed sizes and also by the yard. Some craft shops sell batting scraps by the bag which can be used for stuffing small craft projects. This is ideal for the Teddy Bear Puppet and the Tic-tac-toe game pieces.

Although cotton batting gives a quilt the most traditional appearance, it requires quilting at very close intervals - rows of stitching must be no farther apart than 2 inches. Some cotton batting needs to be pre-washed before assembling the layers, making it a very labor intensive choice and not recommended for beginners.

Polyester batting gives the puffiest appearance. It is lightweight, durable and warm - an ideal choice for quilts that will be tied or tufted.

Cotton/polyester blend batting is the best option because it provides the stability and handling of polyester with the traditional look of cotton.

The batting should be 2 inches larger than the quilt top on all four sides. If you need to piece it to make up the yardage, butt the edges without overlapping them and sew them together using a large cross-stitch.

When assembling the quilt layers, center the batting on the backing and smooth it out from the center towards the outside edges.

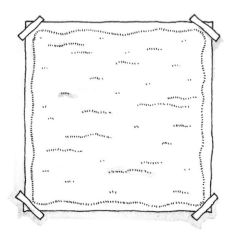

5. ADDING THE QUILT TOP

Center the pressed and marked quilt top on the batting, right side up, starting from the middle. Pin the layers together using long glass-head pins and remove the tape which is holding the backing down.

6. BASTING

A thorough basting job will ensure a beautifully smooth quilt. Thread a long darning needle with light colored thread. Start from the center and baste diagonally to each corner, then across the length and width of the top. Make your stitches about 1 1/2 inches long, avoiding areas or seams you plan to quilt later. For added security, baste a few horizontal and vertical rows in either a grid or concentric rows so that there are basting stitches every 4 inches across the surface.

Baste a last row of stitches about 1/2 inch from the edge on all four sides of the quilt before removing the pins.

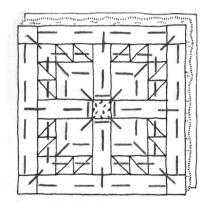

Finally, to protect the edges from fraying while quilting, enclose the excess batting by folding and basting the raw edge of the backing over the quilt top.

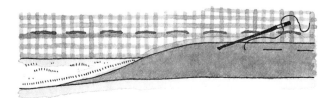

HOW TO QUILT

Quilting permanently holds the three layers of the quilt together and adds depth, texture and visual interest to the quilt.

The quilting stitch is a simple, straight and even running stitch, ideally about 1/8 inch long. In the beginning, do not worry about the size of your stitches; the small delicate stitches will come with practice. Instead, try to make your stitches even, the same length on the top and on the back. Use a **Betweens** needle, size 8 or 9 (the higher the number, the smaller the needle). You may need to experiment a little to find a comfortable length. Experienced quilters claim that the shorter the needle, the smaller the stitch! A flat top metal thimble for the middle finger of your sewing hand is an essential tool.

Thread your needle with a 15-18 inch single strand of quilting thread and knot the end. Choose contrasting or black quilting thread to draw attention to your quilting stitch, or a neutral color to blend with the quilt top. If quilting one of the larger projects, secure the basted quilt in a hoop to hold it taut

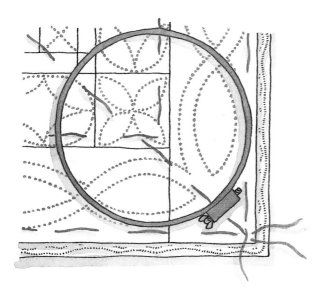

and smooth. Turn the hoop over and make sure the backing is smooth before you begin. Start quilting in the center and work outwards. Do not quilt at random or you will have bumps and puckers.

Hold your quilt in your lap, with your sewing hand on top and your non-sewing hand underneath. Insert the needle

1 inch from where you want to start. Bring it to the surface at the start of your marked quilting line and give the thread a sharp tug to pop the knot through the backing and lodge it in the batting. Make your first stitch using your thimble to help push the needle through the fabric. The hand underneath the quilt feels the point of the needle and helps direct the needle back to the surface to make another stitch.

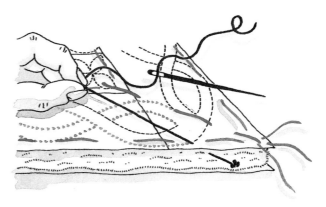

Weave the needle in and out of the layers of fabric in a smooth rocking motion, making 3-4 stitches at a time. You may want to wear a second thimble or Band-Aid to protect your non-sewing hand.

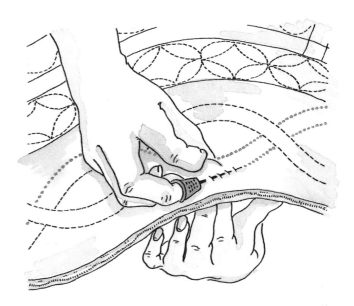

At the end of a length of thread, make a backstitch through the top only. Double knot the thread close to the surface of the quilt. Insert the needle again close to your last stitch, but do not let it go through to the backing. Run the needle through the batting 1 inch away from the quilting line.

Pull on the thread to pop the knot inside the batting. Carefully clip the thread end close to the quilt top.

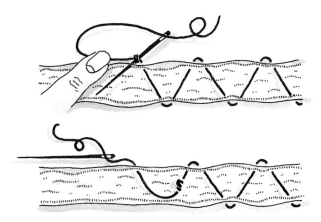

MACHINE QUILTING

Machine quilting is recommended for several projects, where fabrics are too heavy to quilt by hand, and for projects that feature in-the-ditch quilting where the stitching cannot be differentiated from hand quilting.

To quilt by machine, use a heavier needle (No.14), adjust your tension so that it is slightly looser and set the stitch length for 8-10 stitches per inch.

Place the project under the presser foot and place one hand on either side of the seam you want to sew. As you slowly stitch, spread the seam open to let the needle sink into the seam line.

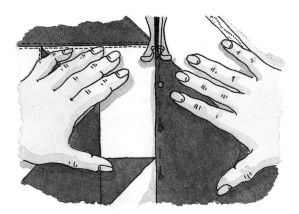

Plan your design so that you can sew continuously. Each time you stop and start a line of stitching you will need to pull your thread ends to the wrong side. Knot them and bury the knots in the batting.

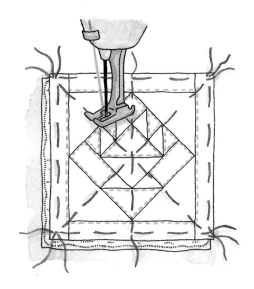

TYING

Tying or tufting is an alternative and much quicker method of holding together the three layers of a quilt sandwich. It is a practical choice for quilts which will require frequent laundering. Using this method, the quilt is fastened at wide intervals so it is essential that you use a polyester batting. Cotton batting will shift and go lumpy unless quilted very closely.

Tying does not require basting. The layers can be temporarily secured with either long straight pins or safety pins approximately every 3 inches apart and at the points where you intend to place a tie.

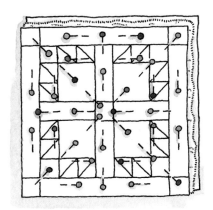

Thread a large-eyed needle with a length of crochet cotton, embroidery floss or pearl cotton. Start with a backstitch over the pin which marks the point you wish to tie, leaving a 3 inch tail. Continue to the next pin, leaving enough slack in the thread to allow you to tie a square knot. Do not cut the thread. Make another backstitch. When you have backstitched over every spot you wish to tie, clip the threads between the pins and tie square knots before trimming the tails to the same lengths.

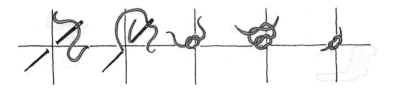

BINDING

Binding is the final stage of making a quilt. It encloses all the layers of the quilt and provides a frame around the quilt top.

SELF-BINDING

This is an easy and economical way to finish a quilt by bringing the backing around to the front. When using this method, the choice of backing fabric is important as it will need to complement the quilt top. It needs to be at least 1 1/2 inches larger than the quilt along each edge.

1. Trim down the batting, leaving 1/2 inch to extend from under the quilt top all the way around.

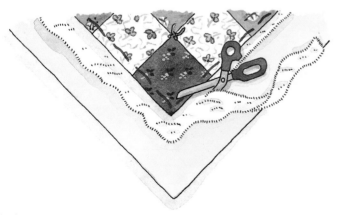

2. Trim away the backing so that 1 1/2 inches extends from the cut edge of the batting on all four sides.

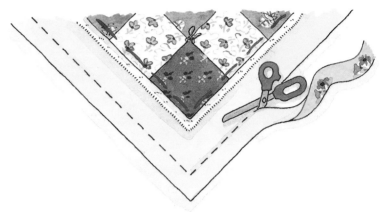

3. Trim off the corners as illustrated before folding the raw edge of the backing in to meet the batting.

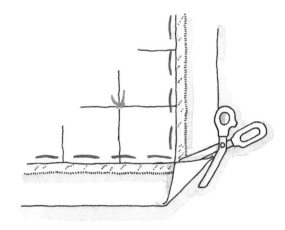

4. Working one side at a time, bring the folded edge of the backing around to the front of the quilt top.

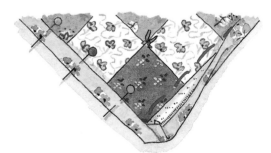

5. Pin the folded edge in place and pin each corner into a neat miter.
6. Finally, use a slipstitch to secure the folded edge of the backing to the quilt top and to finish each miter.

SEPARATE BINDING

This is made up of fabric strips cut across the straight grain and sewn into a continuous length. For wear and durability it is best to use the same weight material for the binding as the quilt top.

1. Cut your binding strips twice the finished width plus 5/8 inch, which allows for two 1/4 inch seams and a minimal 1/8 inch extra for the loft of the batting inside. The finished width of your binding should suit the proportions of your project. Although this decision is very much a personal preference, most quiltmakers opt for a maximum finished width of 3/4 inch.

2. Join the fabric strips together along the short edges to make one length which should be the sum of all four sides, plus an extra 12 inches to allow for corners and overlapping.

3. Press the binding in half lengthwise with wrong sides together. Open up the fold. Turn in and press 1/4 inch of one raw edge to the wrong side.

4. Pin the binding to the quilt top in the middle of one side with right sides together and raw edges matching. Fold in the short end of the binding 1/2 inch at the starting point.

5. Stitch the binding to the quilt through all layers, beginning with a backstitch. Use the standard 1/4 inch seam allowance.

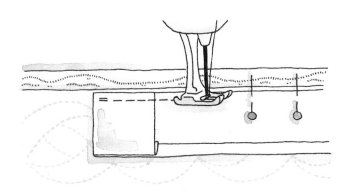

6. Stop sewing 1/4 inch away from the first corner, backstitch, and cut the threads to remove your work from under the presser foot.

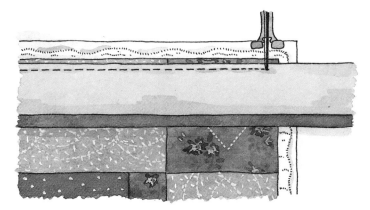

7. Fold the binding strip up at a 45 degree angle, then bring it down to align it with the adjacent edge of the quilt top as illustrated. This step can be a little tricky, but it is important to make a fold or pleat along the top edge to give you the fullness required to fit around the corners, as you fold the binding around to the back.

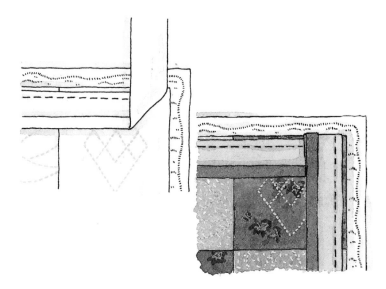

8. Continue sewing the binding to the quilt following this sequence at each corner. As you approach the beginning, allow 1 inch to extend and overlap the folded back section at the beginning. Backstitch at the join.

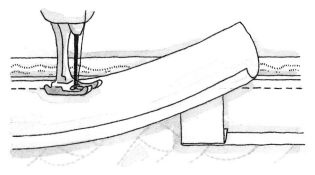

9. Trim away the excess batting and backing before wrapping the folded edge of the binding around to cover the machine stitches on the back of the quilt. Pin, then slipstitch the binding in place.

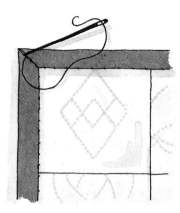

10. To finish the corners, fold in the adjacent sides on the back of the quilt. Stitch the miter in place on both the front and back of the quilt.

When binding curved or scalloped edges you will need to use bias binding and in this case you may find it more convenient to buy ready-made binding. However, be aware that commercial binding is limited in its color range and is also made from lightweight fabric.

STARTER QUILT

To secure the layers of this small lap quilt you will be using an easy and economical technique called tying. Simply, a strong cotton thread is pulled through the three layers, and tied with a square knot. It can be tied either at the front or the back of the quilt and finished with ribbons and buttons. Tying is also known as tufting, tacking and, disparagingly, Methodist Quilting - no doubt drawing attention to the speed in which a project can be completed using this technique. Not only is it a fast way to finish a quilt, it is also hard wearing, permits the use of much heavier batting and is useful for quilts that need frequent washing. Tying is commonly used with foundation patchwork like Crazy Quilts, Log Cabins and String Quilts where blocks are made up of many layers and are too bulky to quilt using the traditional hand quilting stitch.

STARTER QUILT

Skill Level: Absolute Beginner
Finished size: 24 inches square
Finished square: 2 1/2 inches
Total number of squares: 81

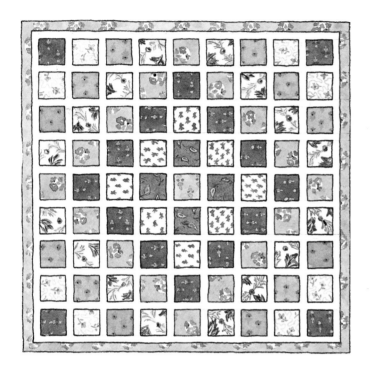

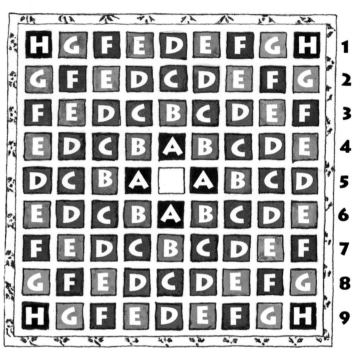

The simplicity of this one-patch, Trip Around the World design, provides the beginner with an ideal opportunity to experiment with color values and with fabric patterns of different scales and densities. Draw the pattern out on graph paper and use colored pencils to help you visualize your design. This will enable you to work out how many squares you need from any particular fabric. Remember, if you want ONE fabric to stand out, use it as the center and then repeat it in several rows.

MATERIALS

- Backing one yard
- One skein of pearl cotton or crochet cotton
- Batting 3/4 yard
- Fabric Scraps (follow the exploded diagram)
Center 1 square 3 x 3 inches
Row **A** 4 squares 6 x 6 inches
Row **B** 8 squares 12 x 6 inches

Row **C** 12 squares 1/4 yard
Row **D** 16 squares cut from the backing fabric
Row **E** 16 squares 1/4 yard
Row **F** 12 squares 12 x 9 inches
Row **G** 8 squares 12 x 6 inches
Row **H** 4 squares cut from the same fabric as row **C**
- Template plastic or tracing paper, cardboard and glue

CUTTING OUT

✄ This project is made up of 81 squares which measure 3 inches. They can be cut either using the template method or from strips.

TEMPLATE CUTTING METHOD

1. Trace template **A** using your ruler to keep the edges straight and the corners square. Glue the tracing paper to cardboard. When the glue is completely dry, use a utility knife or blade held against the edge of a metal ruler to cut out an accurate and reusable 3 inch template. Alternatively, trace the template directly onto template plastic, again using a ruler for marking and cutting.

2. Place the template face down, on the wrong side of the fabric. Use a hard lead pencil and carefully trace around the four sides to give you your cutting line. Templates for machine piecing include seam allowances, so you can mark pieces next to one another. Use sharp fabric scissors and cut exactly on the pencil line.

3. Choose a dominant fabric for the center and cut one square. Following the exploded diagram, cut a further 80 squares from your fabric selection. Although 81 squares are needed to complete the design, it is worth cutting a few more of each color to give you greater flexibility in arranging the layout.

STRIP CUTTING METHOD

✄ You will be cutting squares from 3 inch wide strips cut across the straight grain of the fabric.

1. Fold the lengths of fabric chosen for rows **C**, **D**, and **E** in half with right sides together and selvages matching. Press each length. Lay the folded fabric on a hard, flat surface to prepare it for cutting.

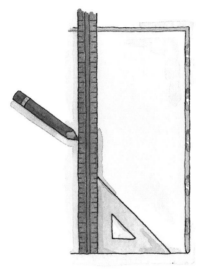

2. Straighten the raw edges using a drafting triangle and ruler. Place the base of the triangle exactly on the fold of the fabric close to the raw edge. Butt a ruler against the triangle. Holding the ruler firmly in place, draw a pencil line along the edge. Cut on the pencil line with sharp fabric scissors.

3. Working from the straight edge you have just cut and without disturbing the two layers of fabric, measure 3 inches along the fold. Line up the edge of your ruler to the drafting triangle ensuring the ruler is parallel to the straight edge, and perpendicular to the fold. Draw a pencil line along the edge of the triangle. Use your ruler to continue the line across the width of the fabric.

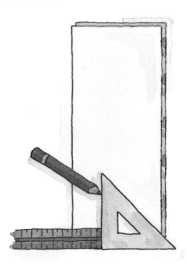

4. Mark another 3 inch strip using the pencil line drawn in Step **3** as your starting point.

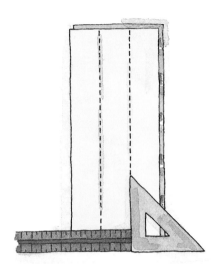

5. Cut out the two strips exactly on the lines.

6. Keeping the strip folded in half, trim off the selvages. Now, cut the strip into squares. To do this, work from the edge you have just trimmed. Align the base of the triangle with the straight raw edge of the strip and measure out seven 3 inch intervals. Draw pencil lines against the edge of your triangle. Before cutting on the lines, pin the two layers together. Make sure your squares are cut accurately by measuring each side and using the drafting triangle to check the corners.

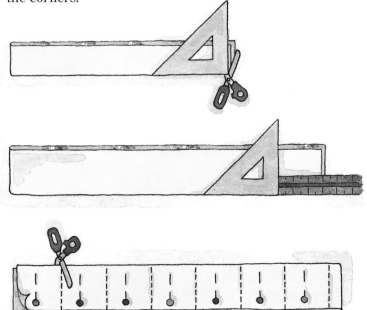

7. Repeat the above steps for the other two lengths of fabric you pressed in Step **1**. From each strip you will get 14 squares. Put each set of cut squares into an envelope and label.

8. Follow the measuring, marking and cutting procedure outlined above to cut the four squares needed for both rows **A** and **H**. Continue with the two 12 x 6 inch pieces of fabric for rows **B** and **G**. Finally, cut 12 squares for row **F** from the 12 x 9 inch piece of fabric.

SEWING THE SQUARES TOGETHER

✂ For position only, pin the squares together in horizontal rows. Starting with the top row label them 1 to 9.

1. These patches have no marked seam lines and have been cut to include an exact ¼ inch seam allowance on all sides. Practice sewing a test seam using the edge of your presser foot as a seam gauge. Line up the edge of the fabric with the right-hand edge of the presser foot. Now measure your seam. If the distance is not ¼ inch, you will need to measure ¼ inch from the needle and place several layers of masking tape on the throat plate to use as your sewing guide.

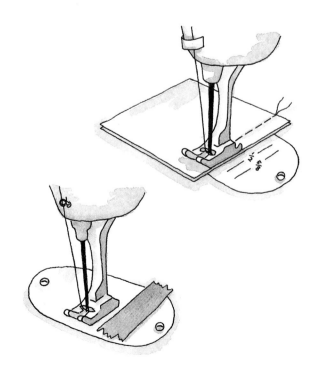

2. Work with one row at a time in sequence, according to the arrangement you have chosen. Pin two of the squares to be sewn, right sides together and all edges matching, with the pins at right angles to the seam line. As you sew the seam from raw edge to raw edge, remove the pins. Stitching over pins can leave your sewing machine needle with burrs and can damage your fabric. For quicker chain piecing, feed pairs of squares one after the other under the presser foot

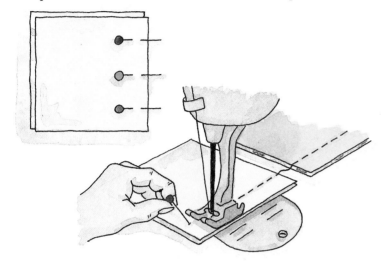

without cutting the thread. After all the pairs have been sewn, snip the joining threads.

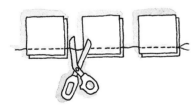

3. Continue joining squares until you have nine rows of nine squares each. Press the seam allowances in opposite directions from row to row.

4. Join the rows in sequence, aligning the alternately pressed seam allowances.

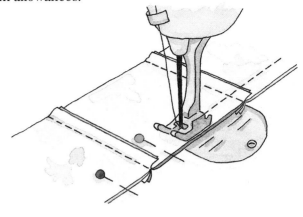

FINISHING

✄ Now that the quilt top is complete, it is time to assemble the three layers in preparation for quilting.

1. Press the quilt top carefully. Snip off any loose threads that may show through to the front of the quilt.

2. Press the quilt backing. Tape the corners down to a flat surface, wrong side up.

3. Center the batting on top of the backing and smooth it out from the center to the sides.

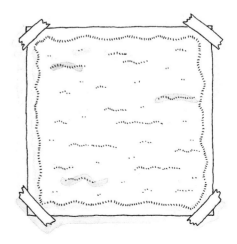

4. Place the pieced quilt top, right side up, in the center of the batting. Smooth the top down over the batting but do not stretch it.

5. Pin-baste through all three layers with safety pins or straight pins at 3 inch intervals so the layers do not shift while tying.

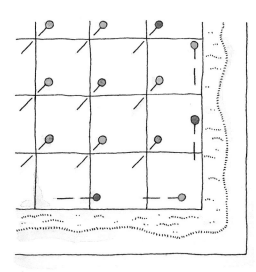

6. Thread a darning needle with a length of pearl cotton, yarn or crochet cotton. Do not knot the end of the thread. Make two backstitches at each corner of the center square and leave a 2-3 inch long tail. Continue onto the next square without cutting the thread. Make sure to leave plenty of slack between stitches. Without snipping off the tail, continue until each corner of each square is threaded.

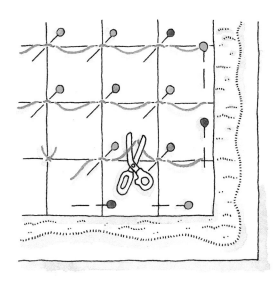

7. Clip the thread between the stitches, then tie the tails into square knots (right over left, left over right).

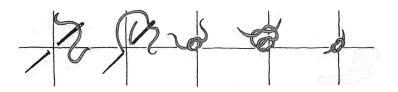

8. Trim the tails to the same length.

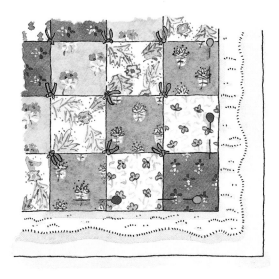

BINDING

✂ Now that the tying is complete, we are ready to finish off the raw edges with self-binding, a simple method of bringing the quilt backing to the front.

1. Using your largest stitch, machine baste through all three layers 1/8 inch from each raw edge.

2. Trim away the batting so that $1/2$ inch extends from the raw edge of the quilt top.

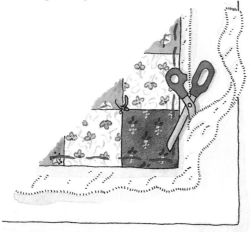

3. Trim away the backing so that $1^{1/2}$ inches extends from the cut edge of the batting.

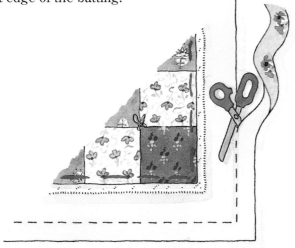

4. To make it easier to miter the corners, fold the backing in to meet the corner point of the top. Trim off the excess fabric at each corner as illustrated.

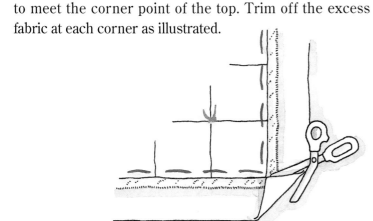

5. Fold and press the raw edge of the backing in to meet the edge of the batting. At each corner, fold in the trimmed edge diagonally to meet the corner point of the quilt top.

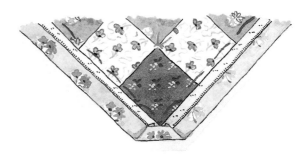

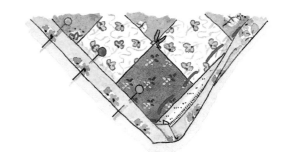

6. Wrap the folded edge, one side at a time around to the front of the quilt. Pin the folded edge in place as you go. Miter the corners by folding the edges in as shown. Pin at the corners to hold the miters together until they are sewn down.

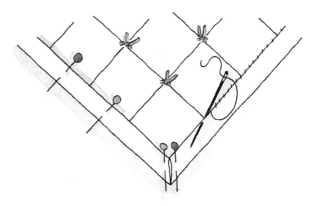

7. Slipstitch the folded edge of the backing to the quilt top using a matching colored thread. Slipstitch the mitered edges together at the corners to finish.

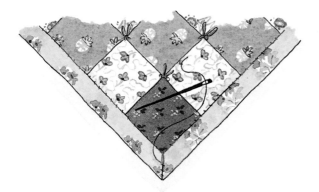

SIGNING YOUR QUILT

✂ Make your quilting project even more special by signing and dating it. If the design permits, pencil the information and embroider directly onto the quilt. If not, then embroider onto a small piece of neutral colored fabric, which you can slipstitch to the back of your quilt.

Made by
Anlee Landman
for
Eleanor Goodwin
25-4-93.

TUMBLING BLOCKS

The scarcity of materials in colonial America forced settlers to be resourceful in
utilizing fabric scraps and recycling worn clothing. Scraps, cut and saved
from old curtains and table linen, skirt hems and woolen suiting were all to be
found in the household sewing basket. These patchwork blocks made
from tiny fabric pieces follow in this tradition of fashioning
domestic items from scraps of any kind.

TUMBLING BLOCKS

Skill Level: Absolute Beginner
Finished Size: 4 x 4 x 4 inches

This simple project incorporates both piecing and appliqué skills and can be completed in an afternoon. These cheerful patchwork blocks will delight young children and brighten any nursery. They are ideal for stacking and building towers with. Additional templates are provided for you to make blocks with a variety of children's motifs. Choose three primary or pastel fabrics and pair each with a coordinating print or check. For the cube itself use soft foam - available from your hardware store - and cut to size with a bread knife or scissors. Alternatively, recycle an old block by simply recovering it.

MATERIALS

- One foam cube 4 inches on each side
- Six large fabric scraps (two coordinated fabrics in three colors)
- Six squares of batting measuring 5 inches
- Fabric scraps for appliqué motifs
- Template plastic or tracing paper, cardboard and glue
- Double-sided tape

CUTTING OUT

1. Using your ruler, drafting triangle and pencil, measure, mark and cut out six 5 inch squares. Draw a diagonal line across each square and cut in half to make 12 triangles.

2. To make reusable templates, trace the six motifs you wish to use onto template plastic or tracing paper. If using tracing paper glue the shapes onto cardboard and cut out. Place each template on a different piece of the scrap fabric. Always position the template with the right side up on the printed or right side of the fabric.

3. Hold your pencil at an angle and keeping as close to the template as possible, trace around each shape. This will be your sewing line, NOT your cutting line. Cut out the fabric BUT add a margin of 1/4 inch all the way round the shape for turning under. Use double-sided tape on the template to keep it from shifting around.

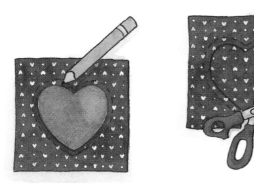

PUTTING THE BLOCK TOGETHER

1. Using the triangles made in Step **1** above, join two triangles along the diagonal edge with a 1/4 inch seam. Do this until all triangles are used up and you have made six squares. Press the seam towards the darker fabric. Cut off the little extra points so that you are left with a perfect square.

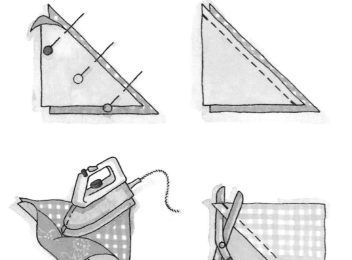

2. Choose which motif you would like on which square. Position the shape right side facing up and pin it in place. Make tiny clips in the margin towards the pencil line, around curves, corners and points to make it easier to turn the seam allowance under.

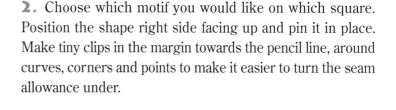

3. Now you are ready to stitch the shape down. Use your fingertips to roll the seam allowance under and gently finger press the edge as you are sewing the fabric in place. Use the tip of your needle to help guide the seam allowance under, just concealing the pencil sewing line. Stitch down all motifs until you have six appliquéd squares. Press.

4. Back each square with a piece of batting and pin the two layers together. Trim away excess batting and baste around the edge of the square.

5. Outline quilt around each shape either by hand or machine. For detailed quilting instructions refer to How to Quilt in the Basic Techniques section. If you are having difficulty machine quilting because the batting gets caught up in the machine, try pinning a piece of tissue paper to the batting as a temporary backing. Simply tear the tissue away after you have finished sewing. If this technique fails, try hand quilting instead.

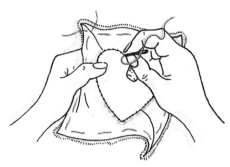

6. Arrange the squares to your liking and sew a strip of four squares, attaching each with a 1/4 inch seam. For each seam, start stitching 1/4 inch from the top edge and stop 1/4 inch from the bottom edge. Backstitch at the beginning and end for reinforcement. This 1/4 inch excess is the seam allowance for joining the top and bottom of the cube.

7. With right sides facing, join the two free edges with a 1/4 inch seam. Remember to start and stop stitching 1/4 inch from each end.

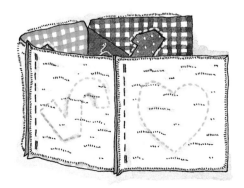

8. Working with the cube turned inside out, pin another square to form the top of the block.

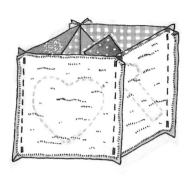

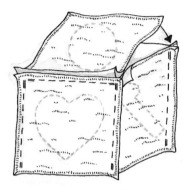

Stitch the top onto the sides of the cube along all four edges.

9. Finally, add on the last square to form the bottom of the cube. Sew along three sides only.

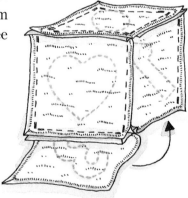

10. Turn the cube right side out and insert the foam cube. Slipstitch the open edge to complete the cube.

BEAR'S PAW CUSHION

The origin of this traditional American block pattern can be traced back to the
Philadelphia Quakers, who called it Hands of Friendship. As settlers
moved westward, the pattern became known as Bear's Paw.
This striking and yet simple motif, with its eye-catching arrangement of
rectangles, squares and triangles, has been pieced together with three strongly
contrasting colors and finished with ribbons on the reverse side.
Every step, from selecting your fabrics to tying the
final bows on the back, will be exciting and fun as you see this
delightful cushion come to life.

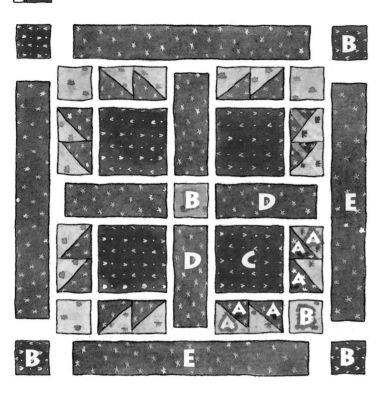

BEAR'S PAW CUSHION

Skill level: Moderate
Finished size: 36 inches square

Although this quilt pattern is made up of 45 pieces, it is deceptively simple to put together. The ease in construction relies on the sewing sequence: first sewing the smallest pieces, then joining them to form rows and finally sewing the rows together to make up the block. This way you are working towards the ideal of longer and longer straight seams. While most projects feature blocks in their more usual dimensions of 6, 9, or 12 inches, in this project you will be piecing an expanded block 36 inches square to make up this giant floor cushion. Instructions for a 12 inches square cushion are given on the final page of this chapter.

MATERIALS

- ½ yard each of two fabrics – light and medium
- 1¼ yards of dark material
- Batting 37 inches square
- Muslin to back the pieced block 37 inches square

- Two pieces of coordinated fabric to back the cushion 36½ x 24 inches
- Ribbons for tying the back of the cushion
- A 36 inches square pillow form

CUTTING OUT YOUR MATERIAL

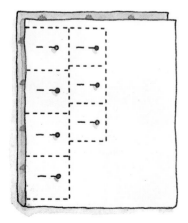

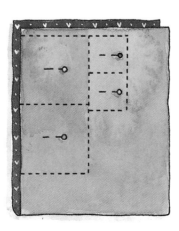

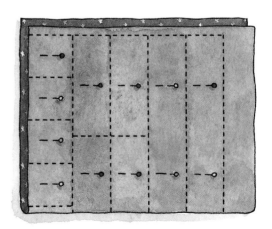

✄ These directions all include a 1/4 inch seam allowance. Prepare each length of fabric for cutting by following the instructions in the Basic Techniques section. Remember: because you are working with the fabric folded in half, selvage to selvage, for every shape cut you will get two pieces.

RED FABRIC

1. Measure, mark and cut two 8¹/2 inch **C** squares.

2. For the corner **B** blocks of the border, cut two squares measuring 4¹/2 inches.

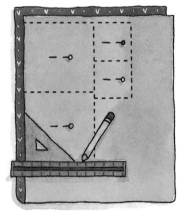

YELLOW FABRIC

1. Cut four **A** squares 4⁷/8 inches. Draw a diagonal line across each set of squares and cut in half to make triangles. This will give you 16 yellow **A** triangles.

2. To make the corner and center **B** squares, measure, mark and cut three squares 4¹/2 inches. You will only need five of the six pieces you cut.

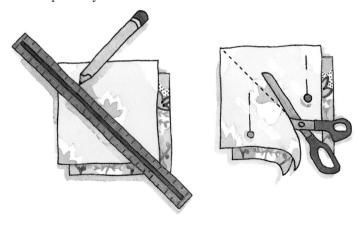

BLUE FABRIC

1. To make the bear's claws, cut four squares measuring 4⁷/8 inches. Draw a diagonal line across each set of squares and cut in half to make triangles. This will give you 16 blue **A** triangles.

2. To make the four dividing **D** pieces cut two strips each measuring 4¹/2 inches wide. Then measure 12¹/2 inches along the strip and cut. Reserve the leftover strips to use for the border.

3. Now you are ready to cut the long pieces for the border. Cut two strips of fabric 4¹/2 inches wide. Unfold them and press them flat.

4. Measure and cut each 28¹/2 inches long. For the other two border strips, use the pieces left over from Step **3** above. Sew them together, then cut down to 28¹/2 inches long.

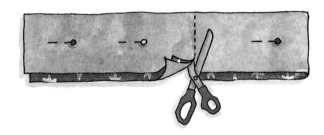

PIECING THE BLOCK TOGETHER

1. With right sides facing, join one yellow **A** triangle to one blue **A** triangle along the diagonal edge with a 1/4 inch seam. Do this until all the triangles are used up and you have made 16 **A-A** squares.

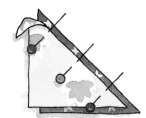

2. Using the steam iron set for cotton, carefully press the triangles open, with the seam allowance towards the blue fabric. Trim off the excess points so you are left with a perfect square.

3. To join two **A-A** squares, place the right sides together and carefully line up all the edges. Make sure that a blue triangle meets a yellow one and that the seams crisscross each other.

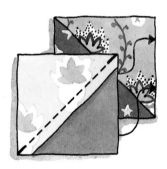

This step is much easier than it sounds, but to make sure you have done it correctly, pin the squares together before sewing. Open up the squares to make sure the blue triangles are on the left. You may need to experiment until your pieces match the diagram below.

Sew the squares together with a ¼ inch seam. Repeat this step until you have four double **A-A** rectangles. Press the seam and trim as before in Step **2**.

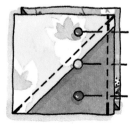

4. Make four more double **A-A** rectangles in the same way, **this time with the blue triangles on the right**. Now take a large **C** square and join it to an **A-A** rectangle along the blue edge. Repeat until all the four large **C** squares are used.

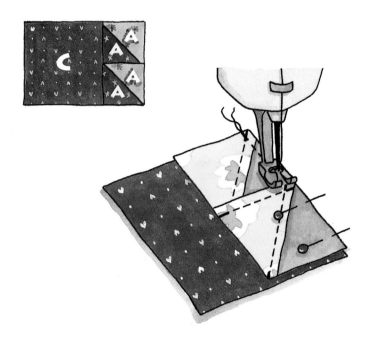

5. Take the double **A-A** rectangle you made in Step **3** (**with the blue triangles on the left**) and add a corner **B** square to the **left** edge. Make three more pieces in exactly the same way.

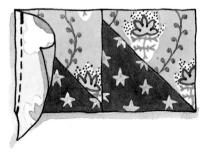

6. As illustrated, sew this unit **B-AA-AA** to unit **C-AA-AA**, to make one of the four paws.

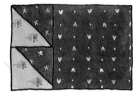

7. Repeat these steps until you have made all four paws.

8. Add a **D** piece to the right-hand edge of a paw and press. Sew another paw to the other long edge of **D**.

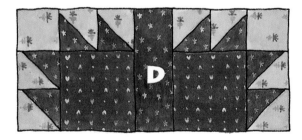

9. Repeat with the other two paws.

10. Make up the middle dividing piece by stitching the short edges of **D** to the left and right of a yellow **B**. Press to the blue fabric.

11. Sew the three sections together to finish the block.

12. Add on the border by sewing a long **E** strip to two opposite sides of the finished block. Press.

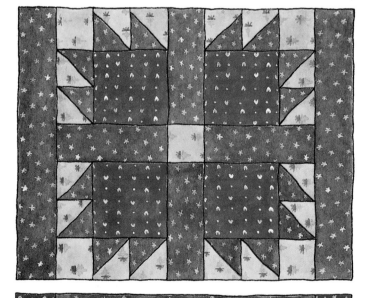

13. Piece together two more 28½ inch long border **E** strips from the remaining 4½ inch wide fabric. Sew a corner **B** square onto each end of the two remaining border strips. Press. Next, sew these two long borders to the other sides to complete the block.

FINISHING THE CUSHION

1. Now that the block has been pieced, press it carefully from the wrong side first. Try not to stretch or distort the seam lines by pushing the iron. Lift the iron and set it down on the next area. Cut away any loose threads which may show through to the front of the quilt. If you are using a quilting pattern that requires marking, transfer the design to the quilt top following the directions in the Basic Techniques section.

2. The backing should measure 37 inches square. Press it carefully to remove folds or puckers. Lay the backing on a large flat surface, wrong side up. Tape the corners down with masking tape so that it does not shift.

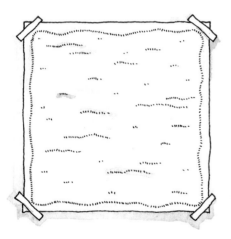

3. Place the batting on the backing and finally the cushion top, right side up. Make sure all three layers are smooth and wrinkle free.

4. Using either large safety pins or long glass-head pins, pin through all the layers starting from the center and moving out to the sides in all directions. The pins should be roughly 8-10 inches apart to keep the layers from shifting while hand basting.

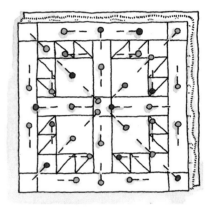

5. Thread a long darning needle with a single strand of light colored thread. Do not knot the end. Start in the center and sew long basting stitches working towards the sides diagonally, horizontally and vertically as illustrated.

6. Continue basting concentric squares roughly 4 inches apart. Although basting takes a little time, it is a preparatory stage that will make quilting easier and guarantee a smooth finish.

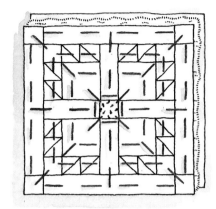

Matching the raw edges, pin the piping cord to the right side of the quilted block as illustrated. Clip into the seam allowance to ease the piping around the corners. Overlap the beginning of the piping by 1 inch and cut away the excess cord. Slip the fabric over to cover the join. Stitch down using a zipper foot close to the cord.

7. Remove the pins. Quilt the block according to your preference. I hand quilted my family's handprints in each of the large **C** blocks, then machine quilted in the ditch to follow the seam lines. Remember that in machine quilting, each time you begin and end a line of stitching, the thread ends must be knotted and secured with the tails re-threaded and buried in the batting. So it is best to plan out your design to enable you to sew, as much as possible, in a continuous line.

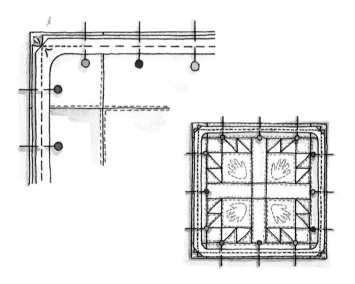

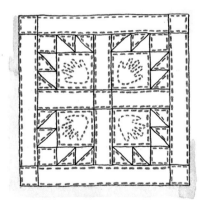

8. Trim all the layers to the size of the quilted block.

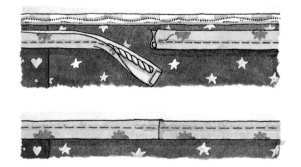

9. To give the cushion a professional finish, you may wish to use piping. You will need 4¹/₂ yards of piping cord. To cover the cord, cut four strips across the full width of the fabric. The width of the fabric strip you cut will depend on the piping cord you choose. Follow the directions for making piping cord in the SASHIKO project. The seam allowance on the piping cord should measure ¹/₄ inch.

10. Now you are ready to make up the back of the pillow. Press a 3 inch hem along the long side of each piece of fabric. Open up the hem and press the raw edge into the fold. Fold over and press to make a double 1¹/₂ inch hem. Each piece of fabric should measure 36¹/₂ x 21 inches. Machine stitch the hem down.

11. With right sides facing, and raw edges matching, pin the hemmed backing pieces to the quilted block as illustrated. The hemmed edges should overlap by about 2 inches. Stitch around all four sides of the cushion, 1/4 inch from the edges. Reinforce the overlap by backstitching several times.

12. Clip off each of the four corners at an angle to reduce bulk and then turn right side out.

13. Slip the pillow form inside the cover through the opening, and stitch three sets of ribbons on either side of the flap to keep the cushion closed. You may wish to use Velcro as a fastening alternative.

MAKING UP A SMALLER CUSHION

If you like the Bear's Paw pattern, but would prefer it on a smaller scale, the block can easily be made to make a finished measurement of 12 inches. Then you can add on borders to suit the dimensions of your cushion.

Refer to the exploded diagram of the Bear's Paw. Using the same letters for each piece, make your own templates to the following dimensions. Keep in mind that these measurements include 1/4 inch seam allowances.

TEMPLATES

✂ **A** $2^5/_8$ inches square and cut in half diagonally
✂ **B** $2^1/_4$ inches square
✂ **C** 4 inches square
✂ **D** $5^3/_4$ x $2^1/_4$ inch rectangle

FOR BORDERS

✂ **E** $2^1/_4$ x $12^1/_2$ inches
✂ **B** same as above

FOR EACH BLOCK YOU WILL NEED

■ 16 light **A** triangles, and 16 dark **A** triangles
■ 1 **B** square for center
■ 4 **B** squares for corner blocks of border
■ 4 **C** squares
■ 4 **D** rectangles
■ 4 **E** border strips

AMISH TABLE RUNNER

The deeply religious Amish communities follow strict rules of plain living, based on simplicity and function. In contrast their quilts feature an unexpected use of vibrant color and fanciful quilting. Their designs are bold, often geometric and frequently use a central motif set inside repeating borders. Today Amish quilts are internationally recognized for their remarkable craftsmanship, beauty and graphic sophistication.

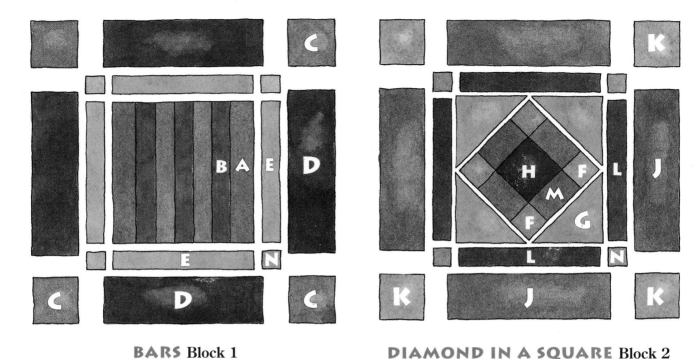

BARS Block 1

DIAMOND IN A SQUARE Block 2

AMISH TABLE RUNNER

Skill Level: Ambitious Beginner

Block Dimensions: 12 x 12 inches
Finished size: 20 x 50 inches

This project combines two Amish patterns which are remarkable for their simple yet sophisticated design: BARS and DIAMOND IN A SQUARE. If at first glance it appears complicated, just take each block apart as you would a puzzle and you will be left with a single central unit. In the case of BARS, this unit is pieced in seven vertical rows. The second block uses a square which becomes a diamond by adding triangles.

MATERIALS

- Light Rose - 1/4 yard
- Magenta - 1/4 yard
- Plum - 3/8 yard
- Royal Blue - 3/8 yard
- Kelly Green - 1/4 yard

- Black - 1/2 yard
- Batting - one piece 24 x 54 inches
- Backing - one piece 24 x 54 inches
- Binding - 3/8 yard

CUTTING OUT

✄ Remember: because you are working with fabric strips folded in half, you will get two pieces for every one cut.

✄ We will be cutting strips of different widths for two different blocks. So to avoid confusion, pin each set of strips together and label as instructed.

✄ Reserve the leftover strips for the optional binding.

✄ Prepare all six quilt top fabrics for cutting. Fold each in half selvage to selvage, press carefully and cut off the selvages.

BLUE

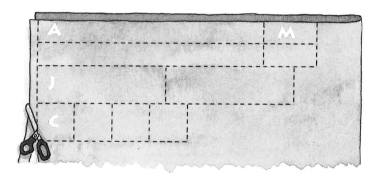

1. Measure and cut two strips 1½ inches wide across the full width of the folded fabric. Using a straight edge, trim ¼ inch off the fold. Then from each strip measure and cut one length of 15 inches and one of 3½ inches. Pin the four short pieces together and label them **M**. Set them aside for **Block 2**. Pin the four long pieces together and label them **A** for **Block 1**.

2. Cut two strips 2½ inches wide across the full width of the folded fabric. Trim ¼ inch off the fold. Measure, mark and cut two lengths of 8½ inches along the strip. Pin the four pieces together and label them **J**. Set aside for **Block 2**. With the remaining strip, measure and cut four lengths of 2½ inches giving you the eight corner **C** squares for **Block 1**.

MAGENTA

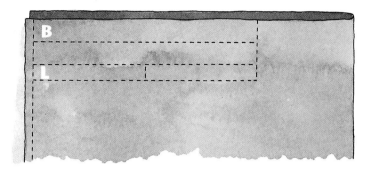

1. Cut one strip 1½ inches wide across the full width of the folded fabric. Open up the strip, press flat and measure, mark and cut three lengths of 15 inches. Pin together and label them **B** for **Block 1**.

2. Cut a strip 1 inch wide across the full width of the folded fabric. Cut two lengths of 7½ inches. Pin and label them **L** for **Block 2**.

GREEN

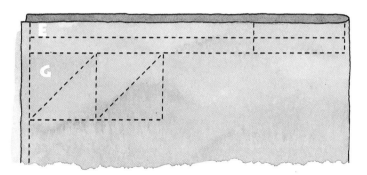

1. Cut two strips 1 inch across the full width of the folded fabric. Measure along each strip from the open end and cut a length of 15 inches and one of 7½ inches. Pin the eight strips together and label them **E** for **Block 1**.

2. Measure and cut two squares 4⅜ x 4⅜ inches. Draw a diagonal line across each square and cut in half. Pin the four triangles together and label them **G** for **Block 2**.

PLUM

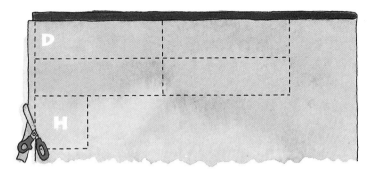

1. Cut two strips 2¹/₂ inches wide across the full width of the fabric. Make each strip four layers thick by bringing the fold up to the selvages. Even up all edges and press. Measure, mark and cut a 8¹/₂ inches length and trim off each end to make four pieces per strip. Pin together and label **D** for **Block 1**.

2. Cut one square 3¹/₂ x 3¹/₂ inches. Label this piece **H** and set aside for **Block 2**.

ROSE

1. Cut one strip 2¹/₂ inches wide across the full width of the fabric. From this strip cut two lengths of 2¹/₂ inches. Pin and label the four **K** squares for **Block 2**. Cut the strip down in width to 1¹/₂ inches and cut two lengths of 1¹/₂ inches. Pin and label the four **F** squares for **Block 2**. Finally, cut the strip down for the last time, to a width of 1 inch. Keep the fabric folded in half and cut out six squares of 1 inch. The twelve 1 inch squares will be used as corner **N** blocks for the inner border of both block designs.

BLACK

1. Cut four strips 3¹/₂ inches across the full width of the fabric. Measure and cut down two strips to a length of 42¹/₂ inches for the top and bottom borders.

2. From each of the remaining two strips cut one length of 12¹/₂ inches for the middle borders and one length of 18¹/₂ inches for the side borders.

PUTTING THE BARS BLOCKS TOGETHER

1. Sew four **A** strips to three **B** strips, alternating the colors as illustrated. Press all seams towards the blue fabric.

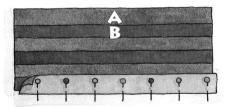

2. Sew a 15 inch **E** strip to each long end of the unit pieced above. Press all seams towards the green border strip.

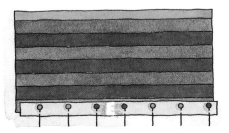

3. Cut the pieced unit into two equal 7½ inch units, using your ruler as shown. This unit forms the center of the **BARS** block. Set one center unit aside.

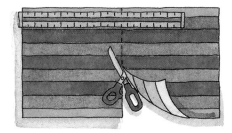

4. Make four **N-E-N** border units as illustrated. Press towards the green fabric. Set two of these aside for the second **BARS** block.

5. With right sides facing and all edges matching, sew the **N-E-N** units to the top and bottom of the center unit made in Step **3**. Press all seams towards the border.

6. Sew two **D** strips to opposite sides of the pieced block. Press towards the border.

7. Sew four **C-D-C** border units. Sew two to the remaining sides of the Block and set the other two aside for the other **Block 1**. Press towards the border.

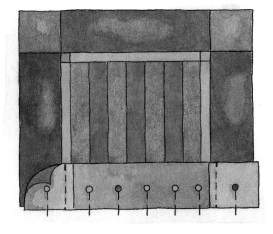

8. Follow the above instructions and make another Amish **BARS** block.

PUTTING THE DIAMOND IN A SQUARE BLOCK TOGETHER

✄ This block is also constructed from the center outwards, adding borders one at a time.

1. Start with the center square **H** and sew an **M** strip to two opposite sides. Press seams towards the blue fabric.

2. Make two inner border units **F-M-F**. Press towards the blue fabric. Then sew these two units to the center square.

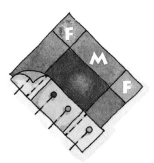

3. Pin, then sew a **G** triangle to each side of the pieced center square unit. Press towards the green triangle after each seam has been sewn. Trim off the excess points.

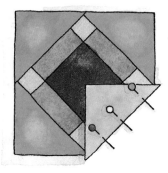

4. Take two **L** strips and sew one to opposite sides of the unit above. Press towards the border.

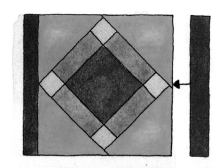

5. Sew two **N-L-N** units. Press seams towards the border and sew onto the remaining two sides of the **DIAMOND IN A SQUARE** block.

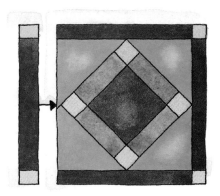

6. Add a **J** border strip to opposite sides of the block.

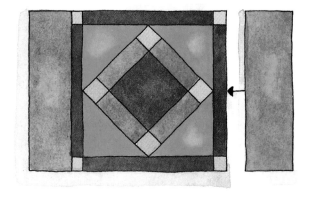

7. Sew two **K-J-K** units and stitch them to the pieced block.

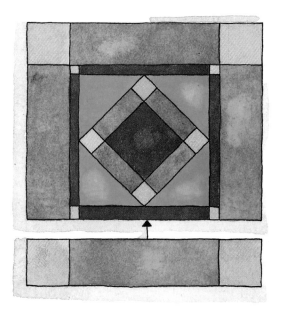

8. To complete the block sew the outer border strips to the top and bottom of the pieced block.

SEWING BORDERS

1. First sew on the two middle 12½ inch borders which separate the blocks from each other. Press seam allowances towards the border.

2. Fold each of the four remaining border strips in half and place a pin at the fold to mark the centerline.

3. Matching centerlines and working out to the sides from the mid-point, pin and sew the top and bottom border strips. Press towards the border.

4. Sew the remaining border strips onto the two sides, matching centerlines and edges. Press.

FINISHING

1. Press the pieced top carefully. Trim off all threads and tidy up the back.

2. Tape the corners of the quilt top down to a hard, flat surface and transfer the quilting pattern. Refer to the Basic Techniques section for instructions on transferring designs.

3. Assemble the three layers - backing on the bottom, batting in the middle and finally the pieced top, right side facing up. Using a darning needle threaded with a single strand of light colored thread, baste the three layers together. Start in the center and sew long stitches working outwards diagonally, horizontally and vertically. Continue basting concentric squares, roughly 4 inches apart. Basting may seem a tedious and lengthy process, but the extra effort will make the quilting easier and give a much smoother finish. Refer to the Bear's Paw Cushion project for basting illustrations.

4. Quilt the top using black quilting thread. Refer to How to Quilt in the Basic Techniques section for detailed instructions.

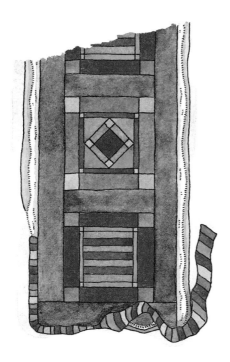

BINDING

1. Sew all the leftover strip pieces together to make a length of 145 inches. Press all the seams in the same direction.

2. Cut the strip down to a width of 2 1/2 inches.

3. Trim the excess batting and backing to 3/4 inch from the raw edge of the quilt top.

4. Now follow the directions for separate binding in the Teacup Quilt to complete your table runner.

CHRISTMAS BOX

The star motif is one of the most popular patterns, and more than 100 variations
have been identified. This eight-pointed star, variously known as
Ohio Star, Morning Star and Variable Star, has been used by quilters since the
latter part of the eighteenth century. It is simply made from a
central square and eight triangles, and is the basis for many other star patterns.
By changing the proportions of the individual elements, by turning
the square on-point or by enclosing the central star within a zigzag border,
a host of new patterns emerges.

CHRISTMAS BOX

Skill Level: Beginner
Finished Box Size:
7 x 7 x 2 inches

In France this all-purpose reversible box is aptly called a vide poche - an empty pocket. It is a simple construction of four borders, stiffened with card, sewn around a pieced star block and fastened with decorative string ties.

This project introduces the Flying Geese pattern as part of the central star motif. It is formed by attaching two smaller triangles to a larger triangle, called the Goose. (See Step **3**, Piecing the Block)

MATERIALS

- Green print for the center 4 x 4 inches
- Paisley print for the border, star points and ties 18 x 9 inches
- Green check for the triangles and squares 12 x 12 inches

- Backing fabric 12 x 12 inches
- Batting - two pieces 12 x 12 inches
- Matte board or stiff cardboard - one square measuring 6 5/8 inches square and four pieces measuring 2 x 6 5/8 inches

CUTTING OUT

GREEN PRINT

1. Cut one **A** square 3 x 3 inches.

GREEN CHECK

1. Cut two squares 3 3/8 x 3 3/8 inches and cut in half diagonally to make four **C** triangles.

2. Cut four **D** squares 2 1/4 x 2 1/4 inches.

3. Cut four **E** squares 2 3/4 x 2 3/4 inches.

PAISLEY PRINT

1. Cut six squares 2 5/8 x 2 5/8 inches. With your ruler draw a diagonal line across the squares and cut in half to make twelve **B** triangles.

2. Cut four **F** rectangles measuring 2 3/4 x 7 1/2 inches.

3. For the ties, cut eight strips 8 inches x 1 1/4 inches. If you would rather use woven ribbons to tie the box, do not cut these eight strips.

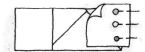

PIECING THE BLOCK

1. Sew two **B** triangles to opposite sides of square **A**. The points of the triangle will slightly overhang the edges of **A**. Press the triangles out and snip off the corners.

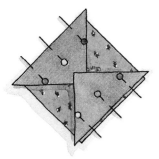

2. Sew two more **B** triangles to the other two sides of square **A** to make up the center of the star block. Sew the seam from one end to the other, overlapping the first two triangles sewn. Press and snip off the corners.

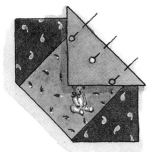

3. Make four flying geese units by joining a **B** triangle to the two short sides of each **C** triangle. Be careful to line up the pieces along the bottom edge. The point of triangle **B** will overhang at the top. Press and snip off the excess points.

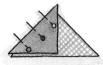
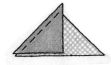

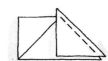

4. Sew a corner **D** square to both short ends of two of the flying geese units made above. These pieces will make up the top and bottom rows of the block. Press.

5. Sew a flying geese unit to opposite sides of the square unit made in Step **1**. Press.

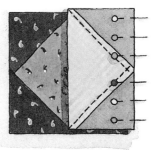
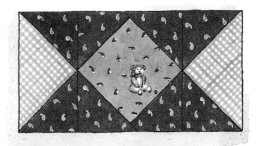

6. Join the three rows together to make the star. Press.

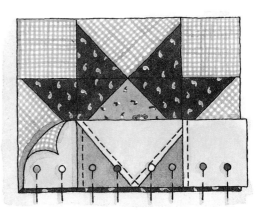

7. Sew two **F** border strips to opposite sides of the star block. Press.

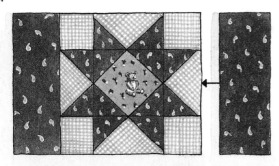

8. Sew corner **E** blocks to each end of the remaining two **F** border strips. Press towards the border. Pin, then sew the border strips onto the star block. Make sure to line up the seam intersections of the corner blocks and borders.

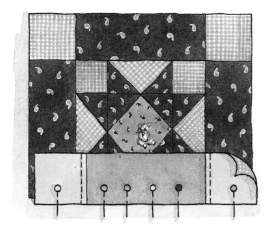

CONSTRUCTING THE BOX

1. Now that the block is complete, baste it to a piece of batting. Following the outline of the star, either machine or hand quilt through the two layers. Refer to How to Quilt in the Basic Techniques section for detailed instructions.

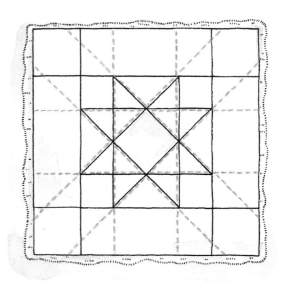

2. Tape the backing fabric to a hard flat surface. Using your ruler and a hard lead pencil mark the backing with a grid of intersecting diagonal lines and baste to the batting.

3. Machine or hand quilt.

4. To make up the eight ties press each strip in half. Open up the strip and press the long raw edges into the center fold. Turn 1/4 inch along one short end before folding the strip in half to make a finished tie 3/8 inch wide. Topstitch close to the open edges.

5. Pin six ties in position just inside the join of the corner border block as drawn.

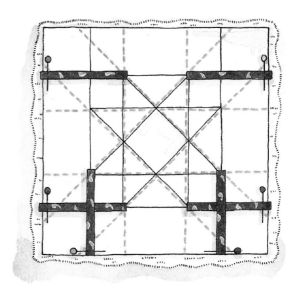

6. Pin the backing block to the pieced block with right sides facing so that the batting is on top. The six ties will be in position between the two quilted blocks.

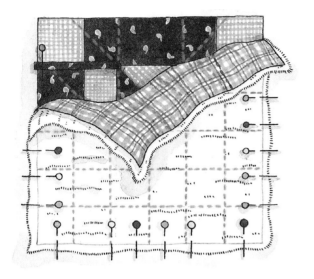

8. Stitch two vertical seams in the ditch between the border unit and pieced block as drawn, stopping 1 inch from the top of each seam. This will create three pockets into which the boards will fit.

7. Sew around three sides of the square using a scant ¼ inch seam allowance. Turn right sides out. Topstitch around the same three sides.

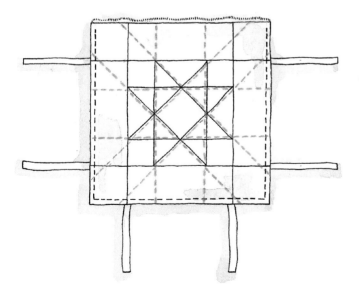

9. Insert the first board and push all the way down the middle pocket. Stitch a horizontal seam in the ditch between the lower border unit and the pieced block to secure the board.

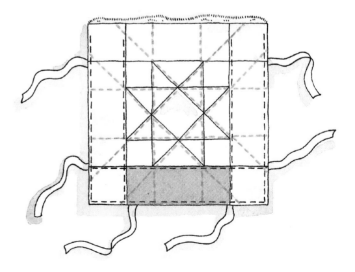

10. Insert two more rectangular boards in the side pockets and the large square board in the middle. Sew another horizontal seam to hold the boards in place.

11. Slip the last horizontal board in the remaining central border pocket. Fold the raw edges in towards each other and insert the last two ties. Stitch the final seam along the top edge. Complete the vertical seams which were left open in Step **8**, backstitching over the join.

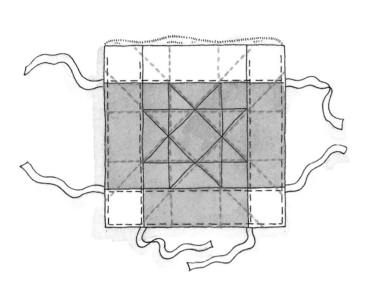

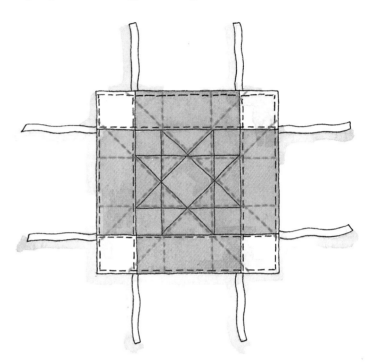

Finish the box by tying the corners together leaving the flaps either inside or out.

BASKET COT QUILT

Whether pieced or appliquéd, filled with fruit or flowers, the basket has always been a favorite motif for quiltmakers. For colonial households, baskets of all shapes and sizes were indispensable domestic items and this may in part explain why they were such a popular subject for celebration on early quilts. A basket of plenty often figured as the central motif on medallion quilts and bridal quilts. Early album quilts abound with decorative appliquéd baskets. Because it could easily be transformed into geometric shapes, the basket survived as a popular quilt pattern when the pieced block developed in preference to appliqué work. The earliest known examples of pieced basket quilts date back to the middle of the nineteenth century.

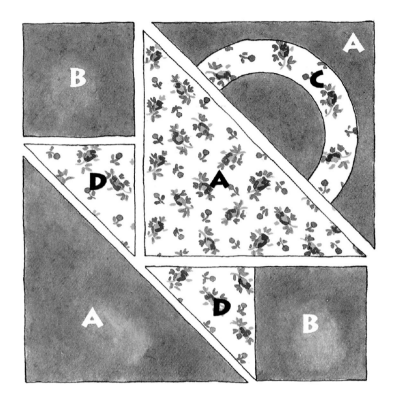

BASKET COT QUILT

Skill Level: Beginner
Finished Size: 46½ x 55½ inches
Total number of blocks: 20
Finished block size: 9 inches

The twenty blocks that make up this cheerful scrap quilt are set next to one another without the visual break of sashing or plain blocks. For this reason, it is important to select a background fabric that will unify the design and give depth to the quilt by providing the necessary contrast in tone. Once your blocks have been pieced, take your time to decide on their arrangement. You could turn the blocks so that their handles all face the center, or change the direction of the handles from row to row. By moving the blocks around, you will discover new designs emerging.

MATERIALS

- Blue background 1¼ yards solid fabric
- Baskets - 20 different prints at least 8 x 12 inches
- Blue check ¾ yards for border
- Red check scrap 11 inch square for corner blocks

- Backing - two pieces each of 32 x 54 inches (excluding selvages)
- Batting - 49 x 58 inches
- Template plastic or tracing paper, cardboard and glue

CUTTING OUT

✂ All measurements for cutting strips include a ¼ inch seam allowance. To cut pieces individually, copy the appropriate templates from the Template section. Trace the solid lines for machine piecing and the broken lines for hand piecing. Prepare all your fabrics for cutting. Refer to Cutting Your Fabric in the Basic Techniques section for instructions. DO NOT trim selvages off fabric chosen for borders.

BLUE BACKGROUND FABRIC

1. Fold your fabric in half, selvage to selvage. Use a ruler and drafting triangle to measure, mark and cut four strips 6⅞ inches wide across the full width of the fabric.

2. Along three of the folded strips, measure and mark intervals of 6⅞ inches. Each strip will give you six squares.

From the fourth strip cut two squares only. Now you will have 20 squares. Save the leftover strip for the 3½ inch squares needed in Step **4**.

3. Draw a diagonal line across each square and cut in half to make 40 **Blue A** triangles.

4. Measure, mark and cut three strips 3½ inches wide across the full width of the fabric. Measure and mark each folded strip at 3½ inch intervals and cut along the pencil lines to make 36 **Blue B** squares. Cut down the remaining fabric from Step **2** to give you four 3½ inch squares. You will have a total of forty **Blue B** squares.

BASKET FABRIC

1. Cut one square 6⅞ inches. Cut in half diagonally to make two **Basket A** triangles. Set one aside for the appliqué handle.

2. Trace the basket handle, template **C**, onto template plastic or tracing paper. If using tracing paper, glue the tracing onto cardboard and cut out your template. Position the template right side up on the printed side of the fabric and trace around the template. Make sure to transfer the center marking of the handle onto the fabric. Adding a ¼ inch seam allowance, cut the outside curve of the handle to give you a semicircle.

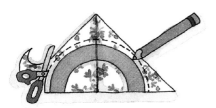

3. To make the two **D** triangles, measure, mark and cut one square 3⅞ inches and then cut in half on the diagonal.

BORDER

1. Measure, mark and cut four strips 5 inches wide across the full width of the fabric.

CORNER BLOCKS

1. Cut four 5 inch squares.

PUTTING THE BLOCK TOGETHER

1. Center the basket handle semicircle onto a **Blue A** triangle. To do this, fold the triangle in half and finger press along the centerline. Now, align the centerline of the handle to the foldline and pin together. Match up the raw edges of the semicircle to the base of the triangle. When you are sure that the handle is correctly in position, baste it in place.

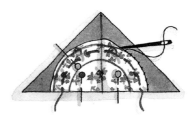

2. Appliqué the top curved edge of the handle using your needle to turn under the seam allowance as you stitch.

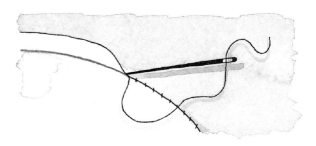

3. Once the top edge has been sewn, cut away the inside curve of the handle 1/4 inch away from the pencil line by sliding your scissors between the background and basket fabric. Be careful not to cut the background fabric. Appliqué the inside curve of the handle. You may need to clip into the seam allowance to get a smooth edge.

5. To make the units for the base of the basket, sew a small **D** triangle to a **Blue B** square. You will need a pair of these units - a **Left Unit** and a **Right Unit**, for each basket block. Open up each unit and press the seam allowances towards the triangles.

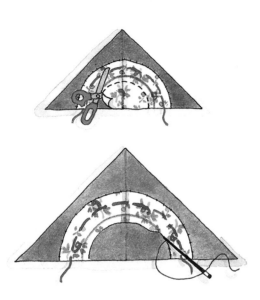

4. With right sides facing and all edges matching pin a **Basket A** triangle to the appliquéd **Blue A** triangle. Sew the triangles together as illustrated, using the standard 1/4 inch seam and snip off the corners.

6. With right sides together and raw edges matching, pin and sew a **Left Unit** to the left edge of the basket. Open the pieces out and press towards the basket.

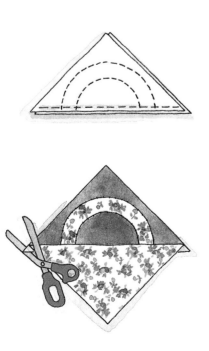

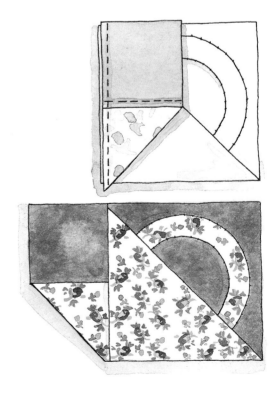

7. Add a **Right Unit** to the other side. Press the seam allowance towards the basket.

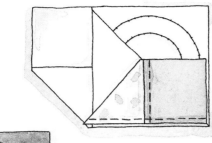

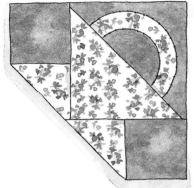

8. To finish the block, join a **Blue A** triangle to the base of the basket. Snip off all excess corners and trim the edges so you have a perfect 9 1/2 inch square which includes the seam allowance.

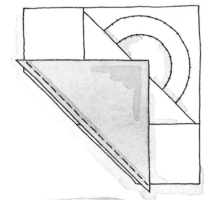

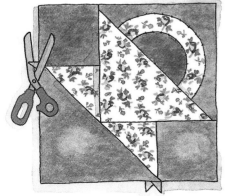

9. Follow the steps above until you have made 20 basket blocks.

PUTTING YOUR BASKET BLOCKS TOGETHER

1. Arrange the blocks on a flat surface, five blocks across and four down, until you are pleased with the layout.

2. Start with the top row and pin the five blocks together with right sides facing. Now sew the blocks into a row using a 1/4 inch seam allowance. Press the seams towards the right. Set the row aside.

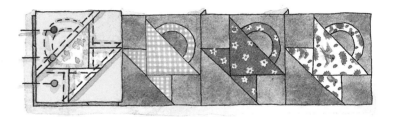

3. Working in sequence according to your design, make up the next three rows. Alternate pressing your seam allowances so you end up with two rows pressed to the left and two to the right.

4. Sew the four rows together to form the quilt top by pinning a row, right sides together, with seams pressed to the RIGHT to a row with seams pressed to the LEFT. Be careful to match all edges. If you have pieced your blocks with a consistent seam allowance the corners of the blocks will match up perfectly.

ADDING THE BORDER

1. Press the quilt top carefully. Measure the length and width of the quilt along the outside edges. Make a note of the measurements across the center. If the two sets of measurements are different, you have either sewn with an inconsistent seam allowance or the quilt top has stretched. To avoid wavy edges you will need to ease the longer sides to a measurement that equals the length of the quilt top measured down the centerline. Use pins to mark the midpoints of all four sides of the quilt top.

2. Using the measurements taken across the center of the quilt, cut two border strips for the width and two for the length. Fold each border strip in half and place pins at the fold to mark the center.

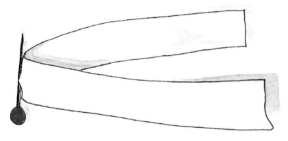

3. Pin the long border strips to the top and bottom of the quilt, matching midpoints.

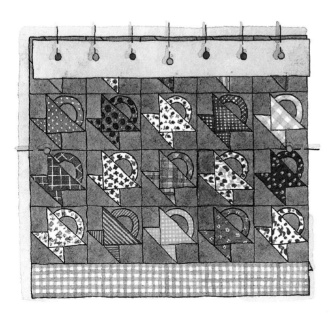

If necessary, ease the fabric evenly out from the center towards the edges. Sew the borders on using a standard 1/4 inch seam allowance. Press towards the border.

4. Pin, then stitch a corner block to each end of the two shorter strips. Press the seam allowances towards the center. Fold the pieced border strips in half and place a pin to mark the center.

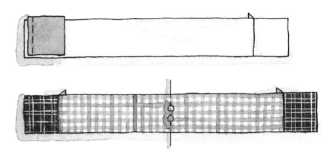

5. Pin the pieced border strips to the sides of the quilt. Match the midpoint pins and make sure that the seam lines of the corner blocks line up with the seam line of the horizontal borders. Sew the borders in place.

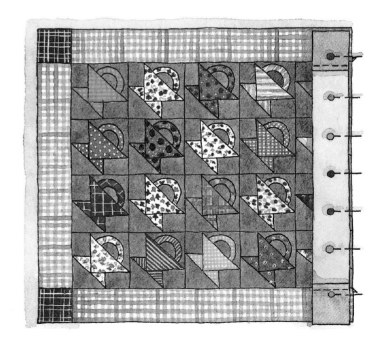

TRANSFERRING THE QUILTING PATTERN

1. Press the wrong side of the quilt top. Remove any loose threads that may show through to the front. Snip off excess points. Turn the quilt over and press again carefully to remove any wrinkles. This will be the last time the quilt will be pressed. Once the batting has been added, it cannot be subjected to the heat of an iron.

2. Make a template of the diamond and circle without adding seam allowances. Remember to cut out the inside of the template as well.

3. Tape the quilt top right side up to a hard, flat surface. Place the diamond template on the border fabric, centering it with the basket block 1/2 inch from the border seam line.

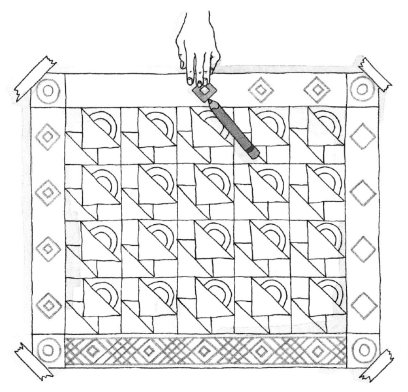

Using a hard, sharp pencil, trace around both the inside and outside of the template.

Following the quilting diagram, continue tracing the pattern until the borders are completely marked. Use the circular template for the corner blocks. You may wish to use a ruler to draw parallel lines to fill in the gaps between diamonds.

4. To mark the square quilting pattern on the basket blocks, align your ruler with the seams following the quilting diagram.

BACKING

1. Use the standard 1/4 inch seam allowance to join two pieces of fabric 32 x 54 inches along the long edge. This will give you a rectangle 63 1/2 x 54 inches. Press the seam to one side.

ASSEMBLING THE LAYERS

1. Assemble the three layers. Pin and baste the layers together following the instructions in the Bear's Paw Cushion.

2. To protect the edges of the quilt top from wear while quilting, fold the backing even with the edge of the quilt, then fold over again to cover the raw edges and batting. Baste the folded edge of the backing to the quilt top.

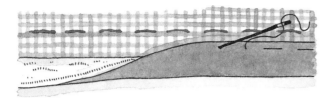

QUILTING

1. Hand quilt the design that you have already marked on the quilt top. Refer to How to Quilt in the Basic Techniques section for complete instructions on hand quilting.

BINDING

1. Remove the basting stitches.

2. For a 3/4 inch finished binding, trim the batting so that it extends 1/2 inch from the raw edge of the quilt top on all sides.

3. Trim the backing so that it extends 1 1/2 inches from the cut edge of the batting.

4. Now follow the instructions for self-binding outlined in the Starter Quilt Project.

TEDDY BEAR PUPPET

In this project you will be making up your own patchwork fabric, from which the teddy bear pattern pieces are cut. From time to time, self-made patchwork yardage and printed patchwork have been fashionable fabric choices for sewing clothes and making furnishing accessories. Early 19th century fabric manufacturers successfully copied and printed fabric to look like the then popular chintz quilts. The 1930's quiltmaking revival also saw a similar resurgence in simulated patchwork, copying such favorite quilt designs as the Log Cabin and Double Wedding Ring.

TEDDY BEAR PUPPET

Skill Level: Easy Beginner
Finished Size: 14 inches

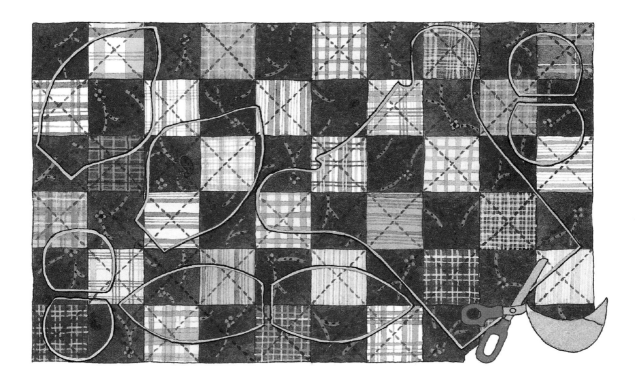

This hand puppet has been designed to entertain children of any age. However, if you intend to give it to a very young child, you may wish to include a few extra safety precautions. Before stuffing the head, the button eyes should be backed by a larger button on the wrong side and sewn through both buttons with a double strand of strong buttonhole thread. It will also be safer to embroider the teddy's nose. Stitch the ribbon to the teddy's neck, secure the knot with several stitches and shorten the tails of the bow. Lastly, double check that you have removed all pins and loose basting stitches.

MATERIALS

- Fabric Scraps - enough to make sixty 2 1/2 inch squares
- One piece of coordinated fabric 10 x 12 inches for the back of the puppet
- Batting 1 yard
- Backing 5/8 yard
- Ribbon 1 yard
- Two Buttons for the eyes
- Embroidery Cotton for stitching the mouth
- Black fabric or felt for the nose
- Template plastic or tracing paper, cardboard and glue

CUTTING OUT

1. Press your fabric scraps.

2. If using the template method for cutting, trace template **R** onto tracing paper. If hand piecing, trace the broken line; if machine piecing, trace the solid line. Glue the tracing onto cardboard and cut out accurately. Alternatively, trace the pattern onto template plastic and cut out exactly on the line.

3. If your scraps are roughly the same size, you can cut three squares at a time. To do this, trace around the template on the wrong side of 20 of the scraps. Use one of the traced scraps as the top layer and place two untraced pieces underneath. Pin the three layers together along each edge before cutting out carefully on the pencil line. If hand piecing, remember to allow 1/4 inch around each piece as you cut. Repeat the procedure until you have 20 stacks of three squares. For scraps of different sizes, cut the squares out individually.

4. To cut squares without a template, use your ruler, drafting triangle and pencil to draw one straight edge from which to start measuring. Using the pencil line as a starting point, measure, mark and cut a 2 1/2 inch square. If some of your scraps are roughly the same size, pin three layers together and cut. If hand piecing, use a ruler to mark 1/4 inch seam allowances on each square after cutting.

PIECING THE CHECKERBOARD FABRIC

1. For quick piecing, use the chain sewing technique as described in the Starter Quilt. The checkerboard rectangle, ten rows long and six rows wide, will measure approximately 12 1/2 x 21 inches. Sew the fabric squares together two at a time with right sides facing until you have made 30 pairs.

2. Snip the units apart and open. Now make up six rows of 10 squares each.

3. Press alternate rows with seam allowances in opposite directions so that the pieces intersect at the correct point. Join the six rows.

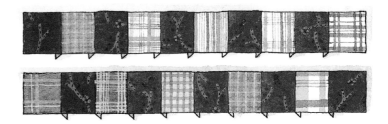

4. Press the checkerboard top carefully, then tape the corners to a hard, flat surface. Using a ruler and pencil, mark out a grid pattern as illustrated. This will give you a reference line when machine quilting later.

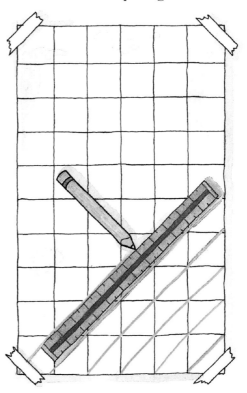

5. Assemble the fabric sandwich - backing on the bottom, batting in the middle and pieced checkerboard on top. Safety-pin or pin-baste the layers at 4 inch intervals to keep them from shifting. Machine quilt along the pencil lines in a matching color thread.

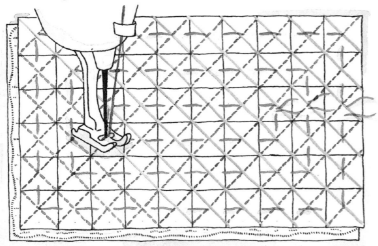

6. Mark the fabric for the back of the puppet with parallel diagonal and intersecting lines, ready for machine quilting. Assemble the three layers and quilt.

PUTTING YOUR HAND PUPPET TOGETHER

1. Trace the pattern pieces for the face, head, ear and body onto tracing paper or directly onto template plastic. If using the tracing paper method, you will need to glue the patterns onto cardboard and cut them out accurately. Label each template and transfer all placement markings.

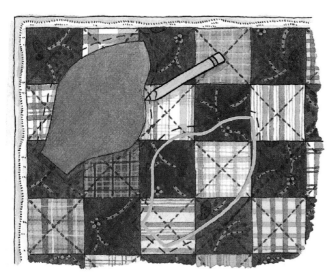

2. Place the patterns on the quilted piece of fabric and trace around each shape with a pencil. This will be your sewing line. As you cut out the pieces add 1/4 inch seam allowances. Remember, you will need to cut out a second face and head with the template FACE DOWN on the fabric to give you the reverse of each piece.

3. Cut four ears from the pieced fabric.

4. Cut out one body from the plain piece of quilted fabric for the back of the puppet.

5. From the templates, transfer markings for center back, center front and ear placement onto the appropriate fabric pieces.

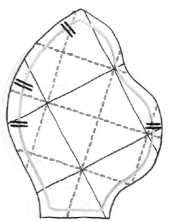

6. With right sides facing and using a 1/4 inch seam, sew the two face pieces together along the center seam. Open out.

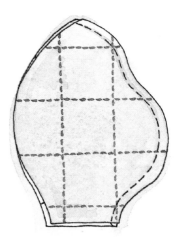

7. Sew together the two head pieces in the same way.

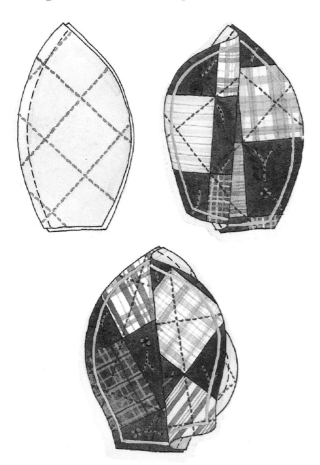

8. Pin then sew, two ear pieces together with right sides facing, leaving the bottom edge open for turning. Make the other ear. Turn both ears right side out, and stuff loosely with batting scraps. Take a small tuck at the base of the ear so the bottom edge measures 1 1/2 inches. Baste along the raw edge.

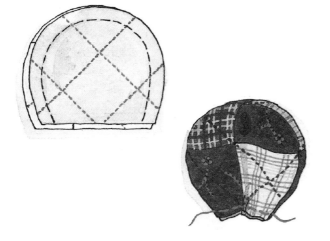

9. Matching raw edges, baste the ears along the top curve of the face unit.

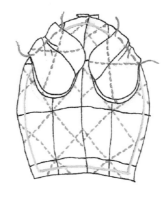

10. With right sides facing, and center seams matching, sew the head to the face, leaving the neck opening unstitched. The ears will be in between the head and face pieces. Turn the head right side out.

11. Now, with right sides facing, pin the two quilted body pieces together. Sew the two side seams leaving the neck and base open.

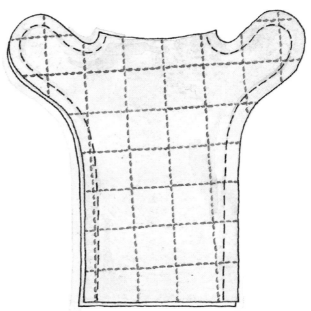

12. Join the head to the body. To do this, leave the body inside out. Slip the head inside the body so that the right sides are facing. The bear should be facing the checkerboard side of the body rather than the plain quilted back. Match the shoulder seams of the body to the side seams of the head. Baste the neck seams together, then sew around the neck several times for reinforcement.

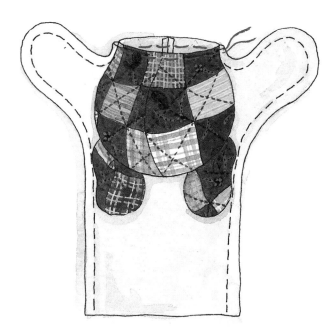

13. Turn the bear right side out and stuff the head firmly with batting.

14. To finish, sew the button eyes in place. For the nose, choose one of the following options: (a) sew on a button; (b) fix a felt circle to the center seam with fabric glue; (c) embroider a nose using embroidery floss of pearl cotton; (d) cut a small black fabric circle and appliqué it in place. Refer to the Basic Techniques section for detailed instructions on appliqué.

15. Following the diagram below, embroider the mouth with stem stitch. Start your first stitch underneath the nose and sew several stitches along the center seam before curving upwards to form the mouth. Finally, tie a ribbon around your bear's neck.

16. Shorten the length of the body to fit and hem along the bottom edge.

SASHIKO BAG

Sashiko is a type of Japanese embroidery traditionally used to strengthen loosely woven indigo dyed garments and to provide extra warmth. The origins of this unique form of embroidery are strictly utilitarian. Today its decorative, geometric patterns inspire quilters all around the world who have adapted it to western quilt making techniques. The inspiration for the stitching patterns themselves are taken from nature - undulating ocean waves, fish scales, hemp leaves and flowers. The pattern featured in this project is called NOWAKE - *pampas grass blowing in the wind.*

SASHIKO BAG

Skill Level: Adventurous Beginner
Finished size: 8 1/4 inches deep
with a 6 1/2 inch diameter

Clamshells and half-moons are the simple and elegant appliqué motifs which decorate this drawstring bag. Because the shapes nest into one another and overlap, select fabrics carefully, alternating light and dark so that the complete motif stands out against the dark ground. The distinctive feature of sashiko is the comparatively large, even stitches, which are meant to resemble grains of rice. Executed in heavy white thread the stitches, 5-6 per inch, are supposed to be all the same length, while the distances between them are kept to a minimum. In traditional western quilting one strives for 10 stitches per inch, with the same distance between stitches on both the top and back of the quilt.

MATERIALS

- 1/2 yard denim or plain indigo cotton
- Backing - one 10 x 22 inch rectangle and one 8 inch diameter circle
- 20 small scraps, roughly 3 x 3 inches
- Eight strips 3 x 1 1/2 inches for making loops
- Lining - 1/2 yard
- Bias binding 25 inches

- Narrow piping cord 25 inches
- Two lengths of cording 30 inches each
- Batting - one 10 x 22 inch rectangle and one 7 inch diameter circle
- Template plastic or tracing paper, cardboard and glue
- White chalk or silver marking pencil
- One spool white quilting thread or pearl cotton

CUTTING OUT

1. Using your ruler and drafting triangle, measure, mark and cut one rectangle 9 x 2 1/2 inches from the denim or indigo cotton.

2. Continue with the indigo fabric and using template **S** trace and cut out a circle with a 6 7/8 inch diameter.

3. Repeat Steps **1** and **2** and cut another rectangle and circle using the fabric you have chosen for lining the bag.

4. Select the eight scrap fabrics you want to use for the half-moons to make up Row **1** in the diagram. Using template **P**, trace the pattern onto the right side of each fabric scrap. The pencil line you have drawn is the sewing line, or your guide for the turning-under allowance. It is NOT your cutting line. As you cut out the pieces, add an extra 1/4 inch all around the shape.

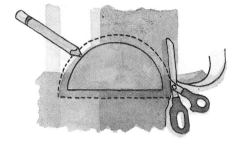

5. Switching to template **Q**, trace and cut out 12 clamshells from your assortment of scraps. Make sure to allow for 1/4 inch turning-under allowance all around the shape as you cut out the pieces.

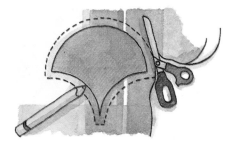

6. For the loops, cut eight strips 1 1/2 x 3 inches.

PREPARING FOR APPLIQUÉ

1. Using the pencil line, fold the curved upper edge of each shell and half-moon towards the wrong side of the fabric. Finger press and make small pleats to give a smooth curve. Baste along the folded edge and press.

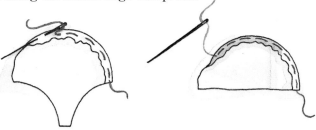

GETTING STARTED

1. Place template **P** 1/4 inch above the bottom edge of the background fabric, starting 1/4 inch in from the left hand edge and trace eight half-moons one next to the other to make up Row **1**. Finish 1/4 inch from the right hand edge.

2. Use template **Q** to mark Rows **2**, **3** and **4** as illustrated. Slip the template into the v-shaped gaps created by the design and trace around the top edge. Trace six clamshells for Row **2**, four clamshells for Row **3** and two for the top row. You should have two pyramids, each with four rows and 10 motifs.

3. Now that the background fabric is marked, you are ready to pin your appliqué pieces in position one at a time. Start at the top of the pyramid with the single clamshell in Row **4**. Pin the clamshell in place so that its sewing line matches up with the positioning line drawn in Step **2**. Its lower edges will be overlapped by the two clamshells below in Row **3**.

4. Use a matching thread for each different colored scrap and appliqué the top curve of the clamshell in place using a blind hem stitch. Loosely baste the lower two raw edges in place.

5. Following the same procedure, pin the next two clamshells in position to make up Row **3**. These shapes will overlap the raw edges of the first clamshell. As before, stitch down the clamshells using the pencil lines drawn on the first clamshells as your sewing line.

6. Stitch down the three clamshells in Row **2**. When you have completed this step, start over with the top clamshell in the second pyramid.

7. Now that all the clamshells are stitched in place, you are ready to sew down the eight half-moons along the bottom edge to complete the design.

QUILTING & SASHIKO

1. Tape the corners of the appliquéd fabric to a hard, flat surface with masking tape. Using template **Q**, trace the nine clamshell shapes in the gap between pyramids to make up the sashiko pattern. Remember to mark the two inner lines.

2. Assemble the three layers - backing on the bottom, batting in the middle and appliqué on the top. Baste the layers together.

3. Outline quilt 1/4 inch inside the arch of each of the 20 appliqué shapes.

4. Use sashiko stitching to follow the pattern marked in Step **1**. The stitches should resemble very even grains of rice - ideally 3/8 inch long with a small (1/16 inch) gap between stitches. Sew with white quilting thread or pearl cotton according to the sequence in the illustration. Start with the motif closest to the base at the right hand corner and stitch the lowest arch. When you finish your last stitch, run your needle through the batting and come up at the end of the middle arch. Continue sashiko stitching along the top curve. Repeat until the pattern has been completed.

5. Trim the batting and backing to the size of the top.

6. Now you are ready to join the sides to make a cylinder. With right sides facing, sew together with a 1/4 inch seam allowance. Press the seam open. If joined correctly, you should have a continuous row of half-moons across the base of the tube.

7. To disguise the seam, trace a pyramid of clam-shells using template **Q** and sashiko stitch.

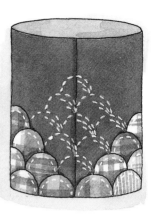

8. Tape the indigo circle for the base of the bag to a hard, flat surface. With your ruler and white pencil, draw a 1 inch grid onto the fabric. Remove the tape and baste together the backing and batting with the indigo circle on top. Sashiko stitch to follow the marked pattern. Stitch around the circumference of the circle to secure all three layers. Trim away excess batting and backing so all three layers are the same size.

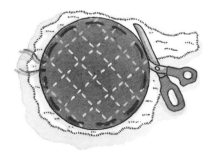

9. Cover the piping cord with the bias binding and pin it around the base as drawn. Sew it in place, making sure to overlap at the join.

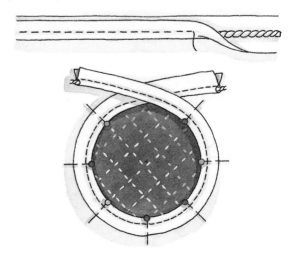

10. Turn the bag inside out. Pin and sew the base to the bottom edge of the bag and turn the bag right side out. Along the top edge, fold and baste a 1/2 inch hem to the inside of the bag.

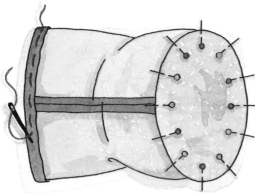

11. Make eight loops from the 3 inch strips. Press each strip in half lengthwise. Open up the strip and press each raw edge in to meet the foldline. Press in half again to make 3/8 inch wide strips, four layers thick and topstitch.

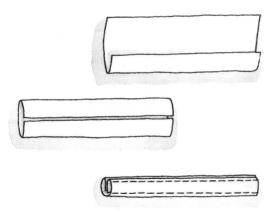

12. Fold the loops in half and pin in place 2 inches apart all around the folded top edge of the bag. Allow 1/2 inch to extend inside the bag. Now baste the loops in position.

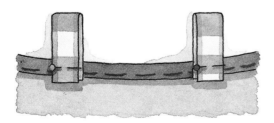

13. Make up the bag's lining. First sew up the side seam. Press the seam open. With the bag inside out, slip the lining over the bag. Fold a hem in the top edge of the lining

and stitch all around to secure the loops and give a neat finish.

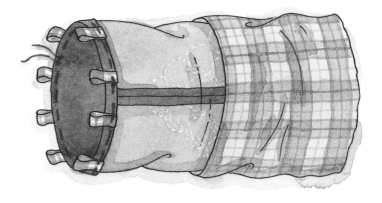

14. Baste through all the layers around the bottom edge of the cylinder.

15. Prepare the lining for the base of the bag by pressing under a 1/4 inch seam allowance to the wrong side. With the bag inside out, hand sew the prepared lining to the bottom of the bag.

16. Thread the cords through the loops as illustrated. Tie knots in the ends and cover the ends of the cords by wrapping them with fabric. Stitch the fabric into the cording.

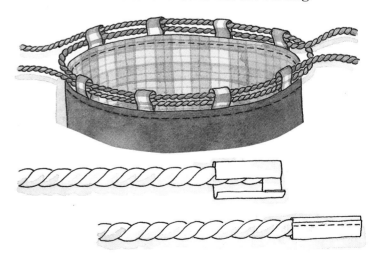

TIC-TAC-TOE

This imaginative fabric version of the tic-tac-toe or noughts and crosses board game is a perfect travel companion. Stars and moons are used as the game pieces and are attached to the board with Velcro fasteners. The quilted pocket on the back of the board is large enough to house the game pieces as well as score cards and pencils.

TIC-TAC-TOE

Skill Level: Beginner
Finished Size: 16 $\frac{1}{2}$ x 16 $\frac{1}{2}$ inches

This project is made as a wholecloth quilt without any piecing. After carefully marking the initial grid either train your quilter's eye by echo quilting squares to make up the game board or trace and quilt squares using the templates provided. The game pieces require careful machining, turning and stuffing and will test your precision sewing skills.

MATERIALS

- Celestial print fabric $\frac{1}{2}$ yard
- Gold cotton backing $\frac{1}{2}$ yard
- Navy cotton 17 $\frac{1}{2}$ x 9 $\frac{3}{4}$ inches for pocket
- Muslin 16 $\frac{1}{2}$ x 8 $\frac{3}{4}$ inches for backing of pocket
- Gold lamé 11 x 24 inches
- Silver lamé 10 x 18 inches
- Batting 2 yards for board and game pieces

- One button
- 10 Velcro dot fasteners
- One spool metallic gold thread
- Template plastic or tracing paper, cardboard and glue
- ✄ Iron-on interfacing $\frac{1}{4}$ yard (only necessary if using lamé for the game pieces)

MAKING THE GAME BOARD

1. Cut two 17 inch squares - a celestial printed fabric for the front and a solid gold fabric for the back. Press the front and tape it right side up with masking tape on a hard flat surface for marking. Use your ruler and mark 1/4 inch seam allowance around all four edges of the square.

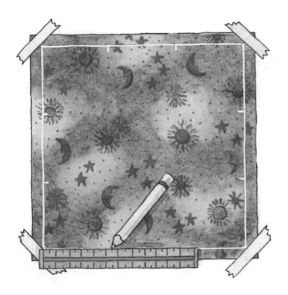

2. Mark a grid on the fabric by measuring 5 1/2 inches from each of the newly marked corners. The four lines will separate the square into nine equal sections.

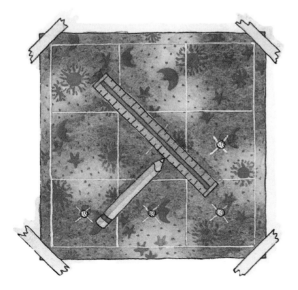

3. Draw faint intersecting diagonal lines across each square to find and mark the center. Remove the masking tape. Either hand or machine sew a Velcro fastener (hook side) to each center point.

4. Make two templates for marking the echo quilting lines, one 3 1/2 inch square, the other 4 1/2 inch square. Tape the fabric square down again to continue marking. Center the templates, one at a time inside each square of the grid. Trace around each to mark the concentric squares that make up the quilting design.

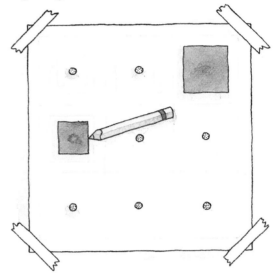

5. To complete the quilting design, mark two parallel lines 1/8 inch to the right and left of the four original grid lines as illustrated.

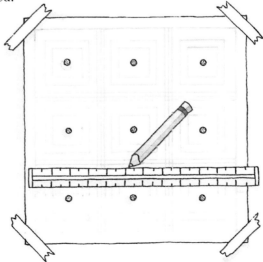

6. To make the button loop, cut a strip 1¼ x 5 inches from the gold fabric. Fold it in half lengthwise (wrong sides together) and press. Open up the strip and press each raw edge into the fold. Fold in half along the original fold and topstitch.

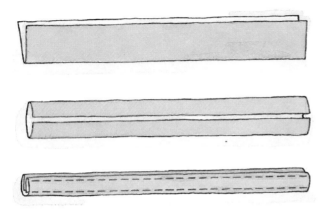

Position the button loop in the middle of one side of the square with the ends side by side, matching the raw edges as illustrated. Baste both ends of the loop in place within the marked seam allowance.

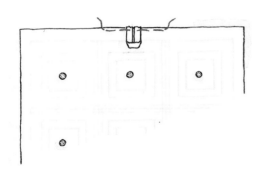

7. We will not be binding this project, so assemble the layers in the following order. Place the batting down first. Next, place the backing and marked top with right sides together on the batting. Pin the three layers together, then stitch around the square using a ¼ inch seam allowance. Reinforce the beginning and end of your seam with a few backstitches. Leave a 4 inch opening in the middle of the button loop side for turning.

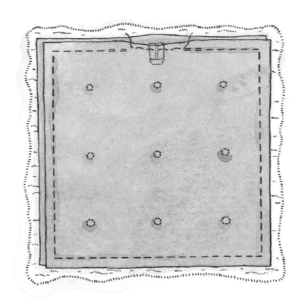

8. Trim around the square so that all three layers are the same size. Cut away the corners to reduce bulk and give sharp corners.

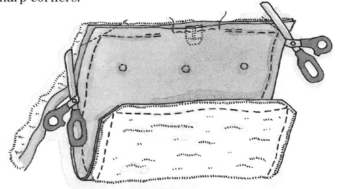

9. Turn the square right side out through the opening. Push out each corner carefully. Press the square very lightly on all four sides. Fold in the raw edges left open for turning. This will bring the button loop to the right side. Slipstitch along the folded edge.

10. Baste several diagonal lines across the game board to prevent the layers from shifting while quilting. Use a double strand of metallic gold thread and hand quilt the marked triple parallel grid lines. Next, quilt the squares within the grid. Start with the middle square and work outwards to each edge.

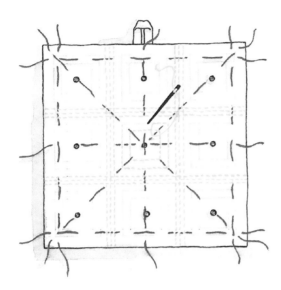

11. To prepare the pocket, cut a rectangle 9 3/4 x 17 1/2 inches from the navy fabric. Tape it down to a hard flat surface with masking tape, ready for marking. From the quilting pattern section transfer the sun and stars to the pocket fabric. Use a white pencil or tailor's chalk to mark the dark fabric.

12. Remove the tape from the pocket fabric. Along the top edge, press a 1 inch hem to the wrong side. Press the raw edge into the fold to make a double 1/2 inch hem. Press a 1/2 inch hem along the other three edges.

13. With the wrong side facing up, back the pocket with a piece of batting and backing fabric each measuring 8 1/4 x 16 1/2 inches. Tuck the two layers under the folded hems.

14. Baste the layers together then quilt the pocket following the marked design with a double strand of gold thread.

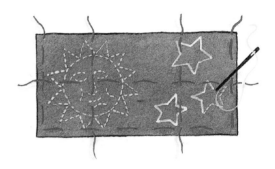

15. Once the quilting is finished, topstitch around all four sides of the pocket. Sew a second row of stitches to secure the double hem. Sew a button in the middle of the double hemmed side.

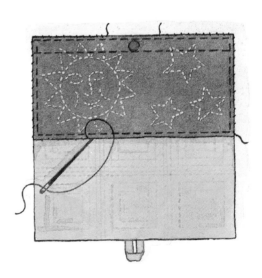

16. Pin the quilted pocket to the back of the block as illustrated. The button edge must run along the outside edge, opposite the button loop side. Blindstitch the pocket in place, leaving a 4 inch opening along the center of the outside edge for inserting the game pieces.

MAKING THE GAME PIECES

1. To make the game pieces, first make templates of the star and moon patterns from the template section. Next, if using metallic or lamé fabric, iron on the interfacing to the wrong side of the fabric following the manufacturer's instructions. Fold and pin each piece of fabric in half with right sides together and press. Using a sharp pencil, trace five moons directly onto the interfacing of the prepared silver fabric. This pencil line is your sewing line. Make sure to allow at least 1/2 inch between each moon for your seam allowance. DO NOT cut out the game pieces until they have been sewn.

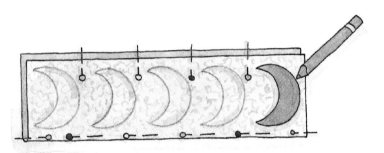

2. Trace five stars as above, directly onto the interfacing of the gold fabric. Be careful to allow enough fabric between each shape for your seam allowance. As before, DO NOT cut out.

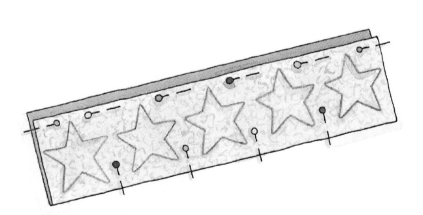

3. Using a very short stitch length, sew on the pencil lines to make five silver moons. Sew very slowly and carefully around the curves a few stitches at a time. On difficult corners

do not use your foot pedal, rather turn the machine by hand for better control. Leave a 1 inch opening for turning right sides out. Backstitch on both sides of the opening.

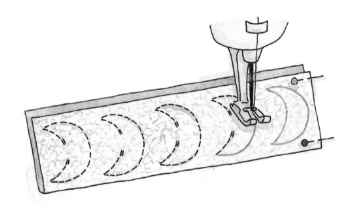

4. After you have sewn five moons, cut away the excess fabric leaving 1/4 inch seam allowance around each shape. Clip into the seam allowance as shown. Turn right side out and stuff with batting.

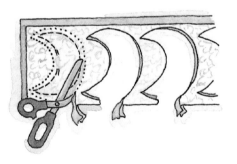

Turn in the raw edges of the opening and slipstitch shut.

5. Sew five stars following the same procedure. Remember to leave an opening along the straight edge of one of the points for turning right sides out. Make sure to backstitch both sides of the opening. At each corner of the star leave the sewing machine needle in the fabric, lift the presser foot, and pivot the fabric to sew the next leg of the star.

6. Cut out the stars ¼ inch from the stitching line.

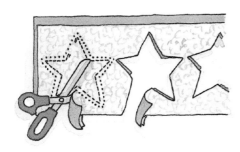

Snip away the excess from the star points and from each interior corner, as drawn.

Turn right side out, stuff with batting and slipstitch the opening closed.

7. Sew the loop side of the Velcro fastener (the furry side) onto each of the 10 game pieces.

HINTS FOR MAKING THE TIC-TAC-TOE GAME

WORKING WITH LAMÉ

Lamé is a brocaded dress fabric that can give a shimmering contemporary look to a project. But because it is loosely woven, slightly transparent and frays easily, it must be backed with interfacing before being cut. Follow the manufacturer's instructions when using iron-on or fusible interfacing. Remember, the dotted or shiny adhesive side of the interfacing must be placed face down, to the wrong side of the fabric.

WORKING WITH METALLIC THREAD

Metallic thread is slightly thicker than traditional quilting thread because it is made by wrapping a fine metal fiber around a polyester core. To quilt successfully using metallic thread, use an embroidery needle or a needle with a large eye. This will make it both easier to thread and also to pull the thread through the fabric. The size needle you use will depend on the thickness of the thread. Since you are using the thread specifically for a decorative effect, follow the instructions for sashiko stitching - larger, even stitches, approximately five stitches to 1 inch, with a small gap between the stitches.

WORKING WITH VELCRO

Most Velcro dots and strips are sold with a self-adhesive backing. When stitching Velcro to the fabric, stay close to the edges, away from the adhesive which will leave a residue on your needle and make sewing very awkward. Also, take care to sew the hook side of the fastener to the game board, and the loop side to the 10 game pieces.

TRADITIONAL APPROACH

If you would prefer the traditional interpretation of the game as noughts and crosses, make the playing pieces using the X and O templates. The game board can be made with either a solid fabric as instructed or by making a checkerboard nine-patch using 6 inch squares.

TOTE BAG

This Cactus Basket design, pieced entirely from squares and triangles, is also
known as Cake Stand and Basket of Chips. It is interesting to
follow the derivation of the pattern names. As settlers moved westward from
the relatively refined, eastern, urban centers to the uncultivated frontier,
quilt pattern names changed to reflect their new landscape and circumstances.

TOTE BAG

Skill Level: Intermediate Beginner
Bag Dimensions:
11 x 11 inches with 4 1/2 inch gusset
Finished Block Dimensions: 8 1/2 inches square

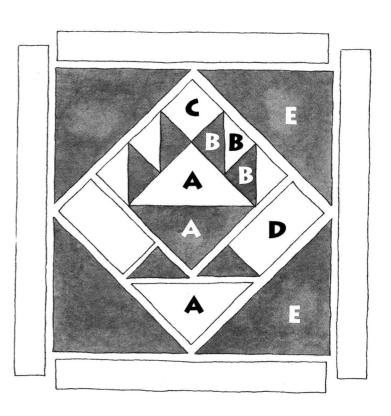

This pieced basket block owes its unique appearance to its setting. It is set on-point, changing it from a square into a diamond. It is a simple 6 inch block, but with the addition of the four corner triangles it appears to float on the blue background.

MATERIALS

- Blue canvas 3/4 yard
- Backing 12 x 12 inches
- White canvas 1/4 yard

- Batting 12 x 12 inches
- Lining fabric 1/2 yard
- Heavy cardboard 4 x 11 inches

CUTTING OUT

✂ Canvas is a heavy fabric and needs to be cut in single thickness.

✂ Refer to Cutting Your Fabric in the Basic Techniques section for detailed instructions on preparing your fabric for cutting.

BLUE CANVAS

1. Measure, mark and cut three rectangles 5 x 11 inches for the bottom and sides of the tote bag. Cut one square 11 x 11 inches for the back. Cut two strips 4 x 18 inches for the handles. Cut one rectangle 6 1/2 x 13 inches for covering the removable cardboard base of the tote bag. Set these pieces aside.

2. For the pieced basket block, measure, mark and cut three squares, $2\,3/8$ x $2\,3/8$ inches. Cut each square across the diagonal to make six **Blue B** triangles.

3. Measure, mark and cut one square, $3\,7/8$ x $3\,7/8$ inches. Cut this piece in half on the diagonal to make two **Blue A** triangles. For piecing the block you will need only one.

4. For the large corner triangles which will set the block on point, measure, mark and cut two blue squares $5\,1/8$ x $5\,1/8$ inches. Cut them in half diagonally to make four **E** triangles.

WHITE CANVAS

1. Measure, mark and cut one square $3\,7/8$ x $3\,7/8$ inches. Cut in half diagonally to make two **White A** triangles.

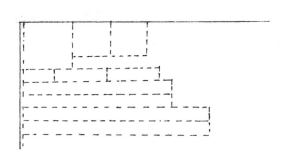

2. Cut two squares, $2\,3/8$ x $2\,3/8$ inches and cut in half diagonally to make four **White B** triangles.

3. Cut one strip 2 x 9 inches. Along the length of this strip, measure, mark and cut one length of 2 inches and two lengths of $3\,1/2$ inches to make one **C** square and two **D** rectangles.

4. For the white border surrounding the block, measure, mark and cut two strips, $1\,3/4$ x $9\,1/2$ inches for the top and the bottom of the bag and for the sides cut two strips $1\,3/4$ x $11\,1/2$ inches.

LINING

1. Fold the fabric in half, selvage to selvage and press. Measure, mark and cut a strip $12\,1/2$ inches across the width of the fabric. From the strip measure and cut a length of 11 inches (this will give you the front and back). Cut one further length of 5 inches (for the two sides). From the remaining strip cut one rectangle that measures 5 x 11 inches for the base of the lining.

PUTTING THE BLOCK TOGETHER

1. With right sides facing, sew a large **White A** triangle to a large **Blue A** triangle along the diagonal edge to form an **A-A** square. Press to the darker fabric and snip away excess points.

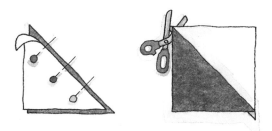

2. Make four **B-B** squares by joining a small **White B** triangle to a small **Blue B** triangle. Snip away excess points.

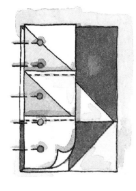

3. Join two **B-B** squares made in Step **2** so that the **Blue B** triangles are on the right. Sew this unit to the top white edge of the large **A-A** square you made in Step **1** and press.

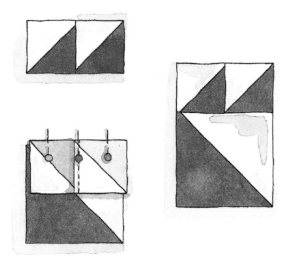

4. Join the remaining two **B-B** squares so that the blue triangles are on the left. Add the **White C** square to the left hand edge and press.

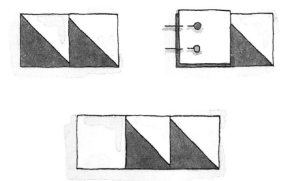

5. Join the **C-B-B** unit made above to the right hand edge of the basket block with all edges matching and press.

6. To make the two base units, sew a **Blue B** triangle to a short edge of rectangle **D**. Repeat this step with the second rectangle, turning the **B** triangle to give you a left and right base unit.

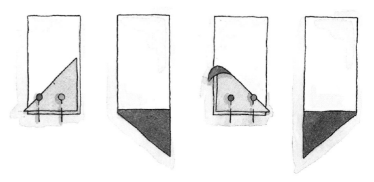

7. With right sides facing and all edges matching, pin and sew the left base unit to the basket block. Press and snip away excess points.

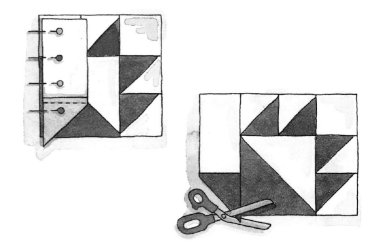

8. Pin and sew the right hand base unit to the basket block as before. Press.

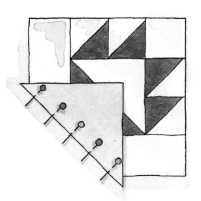

9. To finish the block, pin then sew the remaining **White A** triangle to the diagonal edge. The points of the triangle will extend beyond the base units.

10. Sew a large **E** triangle onto each side of the block, one at a time. Press each triangle open after it is sewn. This step converts the block to a diamond.

11. To add on the narrow white border, pin and sew a 9 1/2 inch border strip to the top and bottom of the block, matching all edges. Press the seam allowance towards the blue fabric. Add on the longer border strips to the left and right sides to finish the block. Press.

12. Snip off any loose threads and tidy up the back of the pieced block. Carefully press.

13. Assemble the three quilt layers - backing on the bottom, batting in the middle and the pieced block, right side facing up, on top. Baste the three layers together with the last row of stitches close to each edge of the quilt block. Machine quilt in the ditch around each shape to give texture and definition.

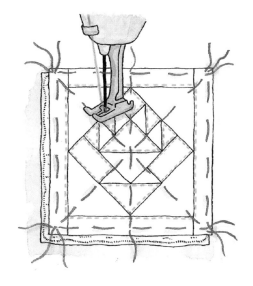

TURNING THE BASKET BLOCK INTO A TOTE BAG

1. Trim away excess batting and backing material so that all the layers are the same size as the quilted block. It should measure approximately 11 1/2 inches on each side.

2. Now you are ready to make up the tote bag. Sew the side panels and back onto the quilted block stopping 1/4 inch from the bottom. Working with the bag inside out, join the back to the remaining side.

3. To attach the bottom of the bag, turn it inside out. Pin the bottom panel onto each of the four sides, then sew one edge at a time, sewing the short edges on first.

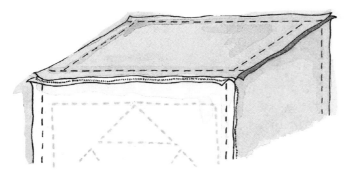

4. With the bag turned right side out, turn under a 1/4 inch seam allowance along the top raw edge and baste to the inside of the bag. The unfinished edges will be hidden by the lining.

5. To make up the handles, press each handle strip in half. Open up along the fold and press each raw edge in towards the center fold. Stitch along the length as close as possible to each folded edge. This will give you a 1 inch handle that is four layers thick and very strong.

6. Pin the handles to the inside of the bag 2 inches from the corners. Make sure to allow 1 inch of the handle to extend down inside the bag. For extra strength, stitch the handle ends as illustrated. Use white thread so that your stitches

are hidden in the white border, and blue thread for the back of the bag.

SEWING THE LINING

1. With right sides facing, sew the two side pieces to the front and back of the lining. Stop each seam 1/4 inch away from the bottom edge. This will give the necessary allowance for attaching the bottom lining piece.

2. Pin, then sew the bottom to the lining, one edge at a time.

3. Measure the depth of the bag. Press a hem along the top edge of the lining fabric towards the wrong side to correspond to your measurement.

4. With the bag turned inside out, slip the lining onto the bag. The wrong sides will be facing each other. Pin the lining in place, making sure that the sides and edges are even. Stitch around the top of the bag close to the edge to secure the lining.

5. Cover the cardboard base with the remaining piece of canvas using tape, glue or spray adhesive. The base should be removed before washing the bag.

SUNFLOWER APRON

During the quilt revival of the 1930's, commercial patterns were produced in
kit form and mass-marketed through newspapers, mail order
catalogues and women's magazines. By 1934, more than 400 newspapers
regularly featured columns on quilting. This sunflower design draws inspiration
from a famous appliqué kit quilt designed by Mrs. Marie Webster,
needlework editor of Ladies Home Journal, one of the most popular and
influential women's magazines at the turn of the century.

SUNFLOWER APRON

Skill Level: Easy Beginner

This attractive and functional apron requires simple sewing skills and introduces you to the basic techniques of appliqué. Classic appliqué shapes - circles, stems, petals and ellipses are featured on a suitably large scale so you can learn the specific techniques for handling points, corners and curves and for turning edges under smoothly. Once you have mastered these, you can attempt more complex shapes and designs.

MATERIALS

- Green twill or canvas for the apron and pocket 1¼ yards (if using fabric narrower than 44 inches you will need to increase this amount by ³/₈ yard)
- Gold fabric for the petals ¹/₈ yard
- Assorted scraps for sunflower center, stem and leaves

- Flowerpot fabric scrap should be at least 10 x 13 inches
- Webbing for straps 3 yards
- D-rings
- Batting - one piece 10 x 12 inches
- Template plastic or tracing paper, cardboard and glue
- ✂ Iron-on interfacing - optional

CUTTING OUT

✄ If using lightweight fabrics for the appliqué pieces, you will need to use iron-on interfacing to give them extra body. Interfacing is readily available from all fabric stores.

1. Select your appropriate templates and from the various fabrics you have chosen cut one sunflower center, eight petals, three leaves and one stem. Remember to add 1/4 inch seam allowances around each piece as you cut.

2. To cut the flowerpot, place the broken line of template **A** on the fold of the fabric wrong sides together. Trace around the template, then cut, adding 1/4 inch seam allowance.

3. For the rim, refold the fabric so that the stripes are horizontal. Position the broken line of template **B** on the fabric fold and trace. Cut out the rim remembering to add 1/4 inch seam allowances.

4. Cut a rectangle 35 1/2 x 41 1/2 inches from the green twill fabric. To mark the curve for the armhole, fold the fabric in half lengthwise, right sides together. Use your ruler and drafting triangle to straighten the top edge and place a pin 7 inches from the fold. With the foldline on your right, place another pin 10 3/4 inches down from the top, along the selvage edge. Connect these two points with a gentle arc, as illustrated, and cut along the pencil line.

5. For the pocket, cut one rectangle 12 x 18 inches.

6. Fold the batting in half and pin together. Place the broken lines of templates **A** and **B** on the foldline and cut. This time do NOT add 1/4 inch seam allowance.

MAKING THE APRON

1. To prepare the pocket, fold and baste down a 1/2 inch hem along the bottom and two sides of the rectangle. For the top hem, turn down ¼ inch to the wrong side and then fold over an additional 2 inches. Press the hem down. Stitch two rows to secure the hem, one along the top edge of the pocket and the other a scant 2 inches down from the top edge.

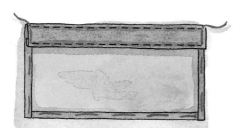

2. Measure 3 ½ inches from each short edge and press a vertical foldline to mark the stitching lines for the side pockets. Fold the pocket in half and place a pin to mark the centerline.

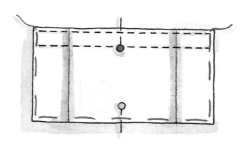

3. To prepare the flowerpot for appliqué, press a ¼ inch seam allowance to the wrong side along the two sides and bottom edges. Press ¼ inch along the top and edges of the rim.

4. With right sides facing and with center foldlines matching, sew the rim to the flowerpot. Start and stop your seam at the edge of the flowerpot. Press the seam up towards the rim.

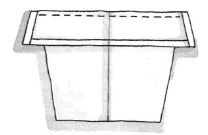

5. Baste the two pieces of batting to the wrong side of the flowerpot and rim, tucking them under the folded seam allowance. Mark the center of the flowerpot base and the rim with a pin.

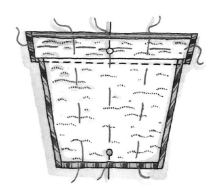

6. Center the prepared flowerpot onto the pocket matching the pins to the foldline. Baste it to the pocket.

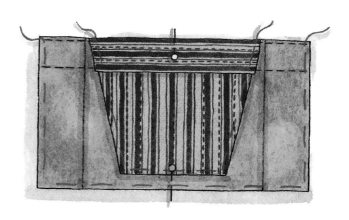

7. Machine quilt with a design of your choice. Refer to How to Quilt in the Basic Techniques section for detailed instructions.

8. Now that the pot has been quilted to the pocket, sew the edges down either by topstitching with a machine or by hand appliqué using a blind hem stitch.

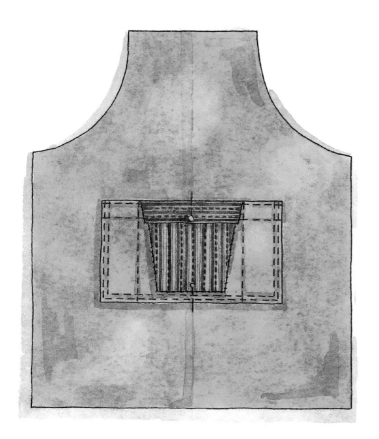

9. Position the appliquéd and quilted pocket on the apron 15 inches down from the top edge along the centerline. Pin it in place, then sew a double row of stitches along the sides and bottom edges. Stitch along the two foldlines to make the smaller side pockets.

10. Prepare the seam for appliqué by pressing under the seam allowance along the pencil line. Pin, then baste the

stem in position. The base of the stem must extend down inside the pocket. Appliqué the stem to the apron.

11. Place the center of the sunflower on top of the stem and baste it down. Arrange the petals evenly around the sunflower face. Tuck the base of the petals under the center. Pin or baste the pieces in position, then appliqué them to the apron.

12. Position, baste and appliqué the leaves to the stem so they appear to float away from the stem.

FINISHING THE APRON

1. For the top hem, turn 1/4 inch to the wrong side and baste down. Measure 1 1/4 inches away from the foldline and fold again bringing right side to right side. Stitch down along the two short edges as illustrated. Turn right sides out.

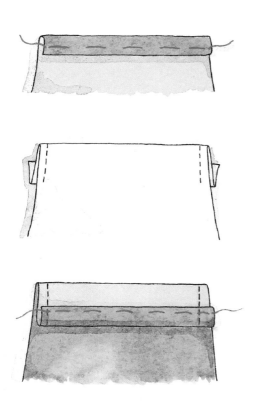

2. For the arm seams, turn under a double 3/8 inch hem along both arm openings and stitch down.

3. For the side seams, turn under and press a 1/4 inch hem to the wrong side. Fold again to make a finished 1 inch hem and stitch down.

4. For the bottom hem, press in a 1 inch hem towards the wrong side. Fold again to make a double 1 inch hem and stitch down.

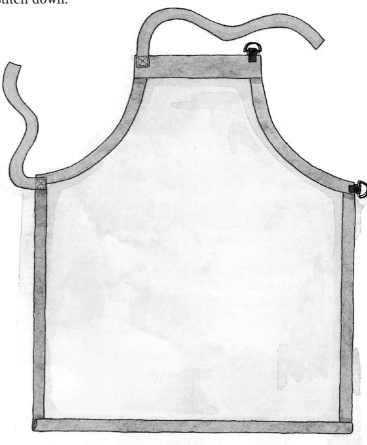

5. Sew on the straps and webbing.

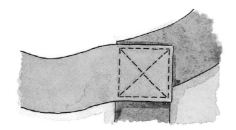

TEACUP QUILT

Best quilts, those made for special occasions or as gifts, traditionally have been appliqué quilts. Early appliqué quilts featured Broderie Perse, a technique in which printed motifs were cut from chintz fabrics, rearranged to make a new design and then stitched to a background fabric. At the time of the Civil War this method was gradually replaced by conventional appliqué in which the seamstress decided on the shape and fabric of the appliqué pieces. The variety of original appliqué designs is endless. The turn of the century saw a thriving industry in commercially designed appliqué quilt patterns and kits.

TEACUP APPLIQUÉ QUILT

Skill Level: Confident Beginner
Finished Block Dimensions: 8 inches square
12 blocks required
Finished Quilt: 43 ½ x 53 ½ inches

Choose glazed floral cotton fabrics reminiscent of fine bone china for the teacups, and coordinating solids or small-scale prints for the saucer and cup liner. When assembling this quilt, you will be using a new technique of setting the appliqué blocks with sashing, posts and corner blocks. The sashing strips and posts separate the blocks and create a lattice effect. An additional frame is created with a wider outer border. The framing of the teacup blocks is an important design element and the success of this quilt depends on careful fabric selection.

MATERIALS

- 12 Floral prints 4 x 8 inches for cup and handle
- 12 Coordinated fabrics 6 x 8 inches for saucer and liner
- Cream fabric ³/4 yard for background
- Backing 1 ³/4 yards
- Batting - one piece 45 x 55 inches
- Raspberry print ³/4 yard for sashing

- Blue floral print ¹/3 yard print for posts
- Pale blue print ³/4 yard for borders
- Dark blue print ¹/3 yard for binding
- Template plastic or tracing paper, cardboard and glue
- One spool neutral colored quilting thread

CUTTING OUT

✂ Refer to Cutting your Fabric in the Basic Techniques section for detailed instructions on preparing your fabric for cutting.

CREAM

1. Measure, mark and cut three strips 8 ½ inches wide across the full width of the fabric. From each folded strip, cut two squares 8 ½ x 8 ½ inches giving you four squares per strip. You will need 12 squares.

RASPBERRY PRINT

1. Measure, mark and cut seven strips 2 1/2 inches wide across the full width of the fabric. Then, starting from the trimmed selvage end of each folded strip, measure and cut two rectangles 8 1/2 inches long. Open the remaining strip and cut it down to a length of 8 1/2 inches for a total of five rectangles per strip. You will need 31 sashing rectangles each measuring 2 1/2 x 8 1/2 inches.

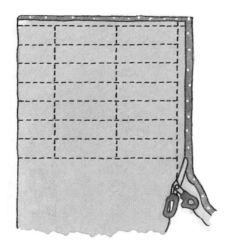

BLUE FLORAL PRINT

1. For the 20 posts, cut one strip 2 1/2 inches across the full width of the blue floral fabric. From the folded strip, cut eight squares 2 1/2 x 2 1/2 inches. From the remaining fabric, folded in half, measure, mark and cut two more 2 1/2 inch squares and two larger squares (for the corner posts) 5 1/2 x 5 1/2 inches.

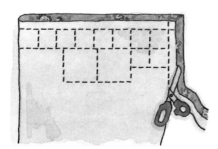

PALE BLUE PRINT

1. For the border, cut four strips 5 1/2 inches wide across the full width of the fabric. Open the strips out, then cut two lengths of 32 1/2 inches each and two lengths of

42 1/2 inches each. Fold each border strip in half and place a pin to mark the center.

DARK BLUE PRINT

1. For the binding, cut five strips 2 inches wide across the full width of the fabric. Join the strips together along the short edge for a total length of approximately 208 inches and set aside.

CUTTING OUT TEACUPS

1. Make templates of the cup **A**, handle **B**, saucer **C**, and cup liner **D** by tracing the patterns in the template section. Transfer all position markings.

2. Press the fabric scraps for the teacups flat in preparation for cutting. Using templates **A** and **B**, trace a cup and handle on the right side of each of the 12 floral prints.

Leave a 1/2 inch gap between pieces to allow for the seam allowances. The pencil line you trace is your sewing line and your guideline for turning under the edges of each appliqué piece. As you cut out the pieces, add a scant 1/4 inch all the way around each piece. Transfer the placement marks for the handle in the seam allowance of the right side of the cup. Finger press the cup in half to mark the centerline.

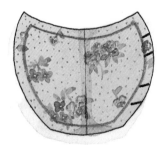

3. Using templates **C** and **D**, trace a cup liner and saucer from the coordinating fabrics. Remember to add seam allowances as you cut. Finger press each piece in half to mark the centerline.

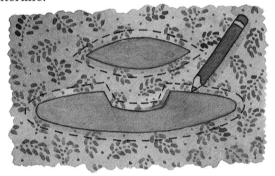

MAKING THE TEACUP BLOCKS

1. Mark positioning lines onto the background blocks by folding them in half and pressing lightly. Press another fold at right angles to the first fold, 2 inches up from the bottom edge of the block. Sew a line of large basting stitches along each fold.

2. Finger press the bottom edge of the saucer along the pencil line. Now, using the basting and center foldlines for placement, pin and baste the saucer in position on the background block. It is very important that the saucer sits level and is centered on the baseline. If not, the other pieces will be off-center too. Measure from the cup inset mark to the bottom of the block to make sure that the saucer is level.

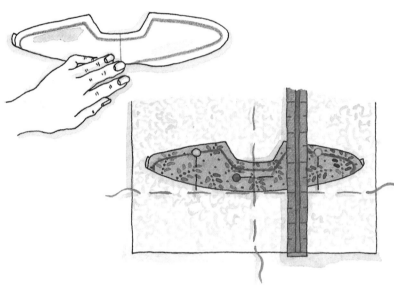

3. Thread your needle with a color to blend with the background fabric. Using the tip of your needle, turn under 1/2 inch long sections of the seam allowance and finger press the folded edge flat. Stitch around the saucer using a blind hem stitch, stopping just inside the edge of the cup overlap. Your stitches should be barely visible.

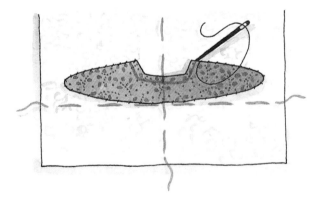

4. Before appliquéing the cup to the block, sew the top curved edge of the cup **A** to the cup liner **D**. Turn under and finger press the top edge of the cup along the pencil line. Matching center foldlines, pin then stitch the folded edge of the cup to the pencil line of the liner. Do not stitch into the seam allowance, but stop at the corners. This will make it easier to turn under the edges of the cup. Press.

5. Turn under and baste down the seam allowance on the bottom edge of the cup. Matching center foldlines, position the base of the cup into the saucer inset. When you are certain the cup is centered on the saucer, baste it in place.

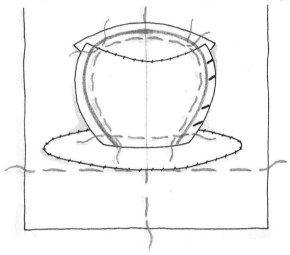

6. Starting at the top right edge of the cup liner, needle-turn the seam allowance under and appliqué the cup to the

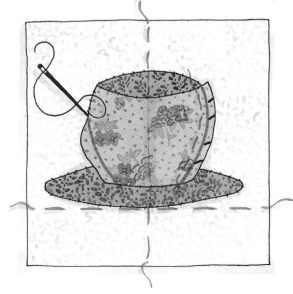

block. Continue all around the left side and base of the cup, leaving the right hand side open for the handle.

7. Prepare the handle for appliqué by finger pressing the seam allowance under. This piece is very narrow and may require you to trim the seam allowance down to a minimum of $3/16$ inch. Baste the handle in position, slipping the raw ends under the edge of the cup. Sew the inside curve of the handle down first, then the outside curve.

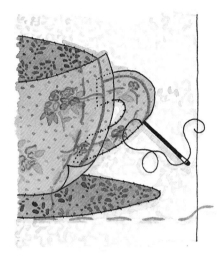

8. To finish the block, appliqué the right side of the cup to the background making sure the ends of the handle are concealed under the cup. Take special care to tuck under the seam allowance where the cup and liner are joined. Remove all basting stitches once the teacup and saucer have been sewn down.

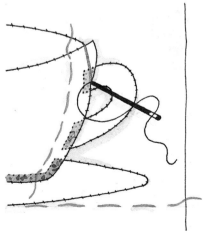

9. Make 11 more teacup blocks following the same procedure.

PUTTING THE QUILT TOP TOGETHER

1. Lay out the 12 blocks in a grid of three blocks across and four blocks down.

2. Sew the sashing strips to the sides of the blocks using a 1/4 inch seam allowance. Press seam allowances towards the sashing strip.

3. To piece the five horizontal sashing strips, sew together three sashing strips to four posts, starting and finishing with a post. Press the seam allowances towards the sashing.

4. According to your layout, alternate a row of teacups with a horizontal sashing row. With right sides facing, pin them together at the intersections of their seams. Sew the rows together checking that the seam lines of the sashing, blocks and posts match up.

5. Press the quilt top very carefully from the wrong side so that the appliqué is not completely flattened. Place a pin at the midpoint of each side of the quilt.

6. With right sides facing, pin the longer border strips to the sides of the quilt. Match center points and work from the middle out to each edge without stretching the border. Sew on the side borders and press seam allowances towards the border.

7. Sew a 5 1/2 inch square corner block to each short end of the remaining border strips. Press towards the border strip.

8. Finally, sew the pieced border units to the top and bottom of the quilt top. Press the seam allowances towards the border.

FINISHING THE QUILT

1. Press the quilt very carefully from the wrong side. Inspect the back of the quilt and snip off any threads or fabric points which may show through to the front.

2. Transfer the quilting design to the borders and corner blocks using the templates provided in the template section. Refer to the Basic Techniques section for detailed instructions on transferring quilting patterns. The center of the quilt will not require marking as it will be quilted in the ditch.

3. Assemble the quilt layers, pin and baste thoroughly. Remember to stitch the last line of basting stitches through all three layers 1/8 inch from the edge all the way around. As a way of keeping the edges of the quilt sandwich tidy while quilting, bring the excess backing fabric around to the front of the quilt top and baste it in place.

4. Read through How to Quilt in the Basic Techniques section for detailed quilting instructions. Starting from one of the center blocks, quilt in the ditch around the teacup, and then around the perimeter of the block. Continue until all blocks are quilted. Quilt the border and corner blocks last.

BINDING

✂ You will be finishing this quilt with separate binding, using the length of continuous binding fabric already sewn.

1. Press the continuous binding in half lengthwise with wrong sides together. Open up the fold. Turn in and press 1/4 inch of one raw edge to the wrong side.

2. With right sides together and raw edges matching, pin the binding to the quilt top, starting in the middle of one side. Fold in the beginning of the binding strip 1/2 inch to the wrong side as shown.

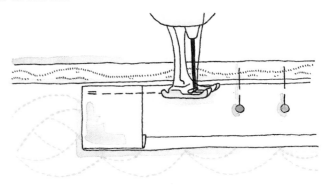

3. Starting with a backstitch, stitch the binding to the quilt through all layers using a 1/4 inch seam allowance. STOP sewing exactly 1/4 inch away from the first corner. Backstitch, snip off the threads and remove the quilt from under the presser foot.

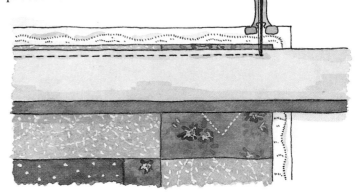

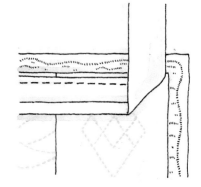

4. Fold the binding strip up at a 45 degree angle. Finger press along the fold.

5. Fold the binding strip down to make a corner. The fold should extend 1/4 inch above the binding. Align the raw edge of the binding with the adjacent edge of the quilt top. Stitch the binding in place starting from the top of the corner.

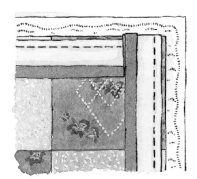

6. Continue sewing the binding to the quilt following the same procedure for all corners. Finish sewing the binding, overlapping the starting point by 1 inch. Backstitch at the join.

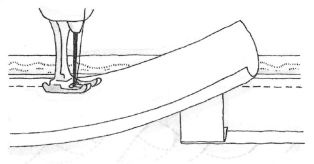

7. Trim the excess batting and backing to 1/2 inch from the raw edge of the quilt top.

8. Turn the work to the wrong side and wrap the binding around the raw edge of the quilt to the back. Pin, then slipstitch the folded edge of the binding to cover the stitching line.

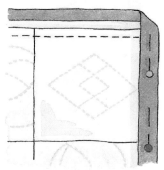

9. Fold and pin the corners into neat miters. Sew several stitches to hold the miter in place on both the front and back of the quilt.

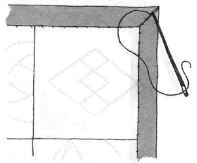

MAKING AND USING TEMPLATES

A template is a master pattern piece made of plastic or durable cardboard used as a guide around which to trace cutting or stitching lines onto fabric.

To make a template, trace the pattern piece you need from this book onto tracing paper or directly onto template plastic. If using the tracing paper method, you will need to glue the paper to cardboard before carefully cutting out the template shape. For more durable templates use template plastic which is available from art supply stores. Trace slowly and accurately with a sharp pencil. Use a ruler to keep lines straight and all corners square.

Cut out the template very carefully just inside the pencil line. Label each pattern piece with the appropriate letter and block name. Also, copy any placement instructions and grain line arrows onto the template.

The patchwork patterns in this book are printed with a solid line and a broken line. If you intend to piece your patchwork by hand, trace the inside broken line to make a finished-size template. Mark around the template, placed face down on the wrong side of the fabric with a sharp pencil. Leave at least 1/2 inch between each piece. The lines you draw are your stitching lines. As you cut out each fabric piece, add 1/4 inch seam allowance on all sides.

For machine piecing, use the outer solid line to make your templates. Draw around the templates on the wrong side of the fabric. Since templates for machine piecing already include seam allowances, mark pieces adjacent to one another. This will give you the most efficient use of your fabric. Cut accurately, exactly on the marked lines, with sharp scissors.

Appliqué pattern pieces are printed with a single solid line. Make finished-size templates by tracing the appropriate pattern and mounting it on cardboard. Trace around the templates, placed RIGHT side up, on the RIGHT side of the fabric, leaving at least 1/2 inch between pieces. Add a scant 1/4 inch seam allowance around each piece as you cut. You will use the pencil line as a guide to turn under the seam allowance and stitch just inside the pencil line on the fold.

For marking fabric, use lead or light blue pencil on light colors and white pencil or tailor's chalk on dark colors. Be sure to keep pencil points thin and sharp so that lines are accurate. Never use a ball-point pen or a marking pen on fabric.

STARTER QUILT

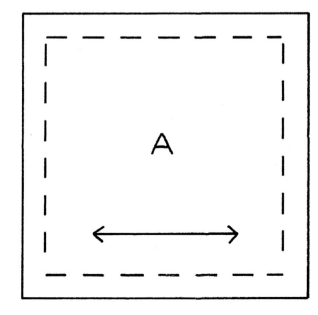
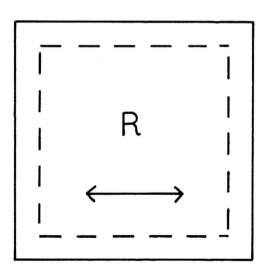

TUMBLING BLOCKS

BEAR'S PAW CUSHION

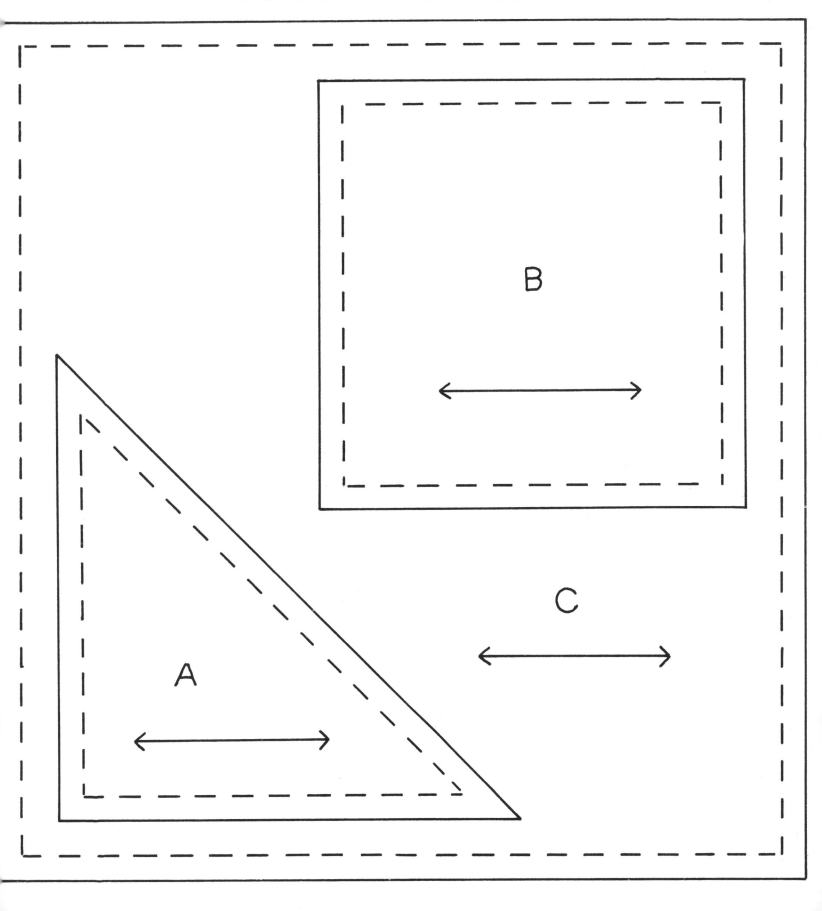

BASKET COT QUILT

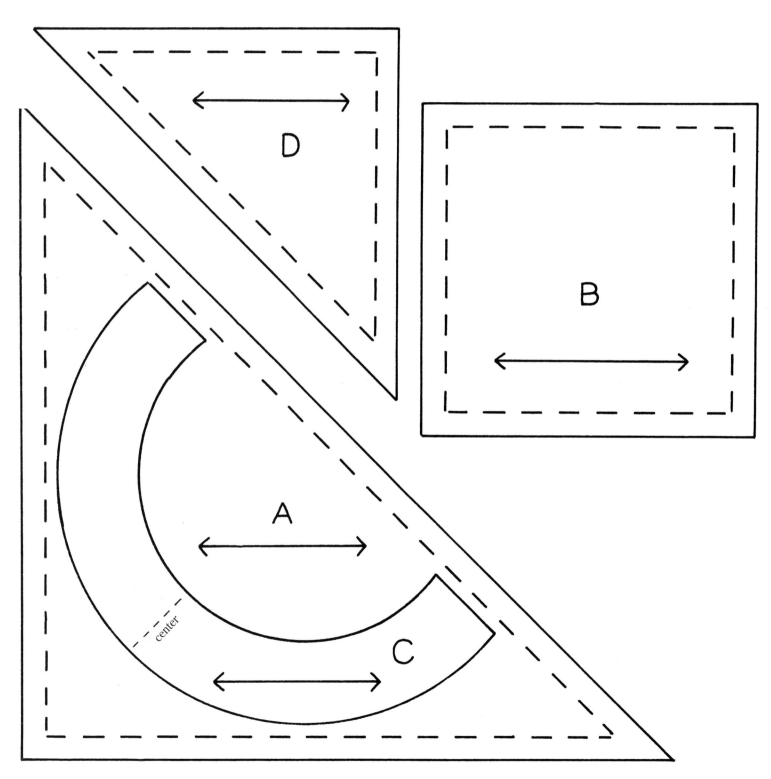

TEDDY BEAR PUPPET

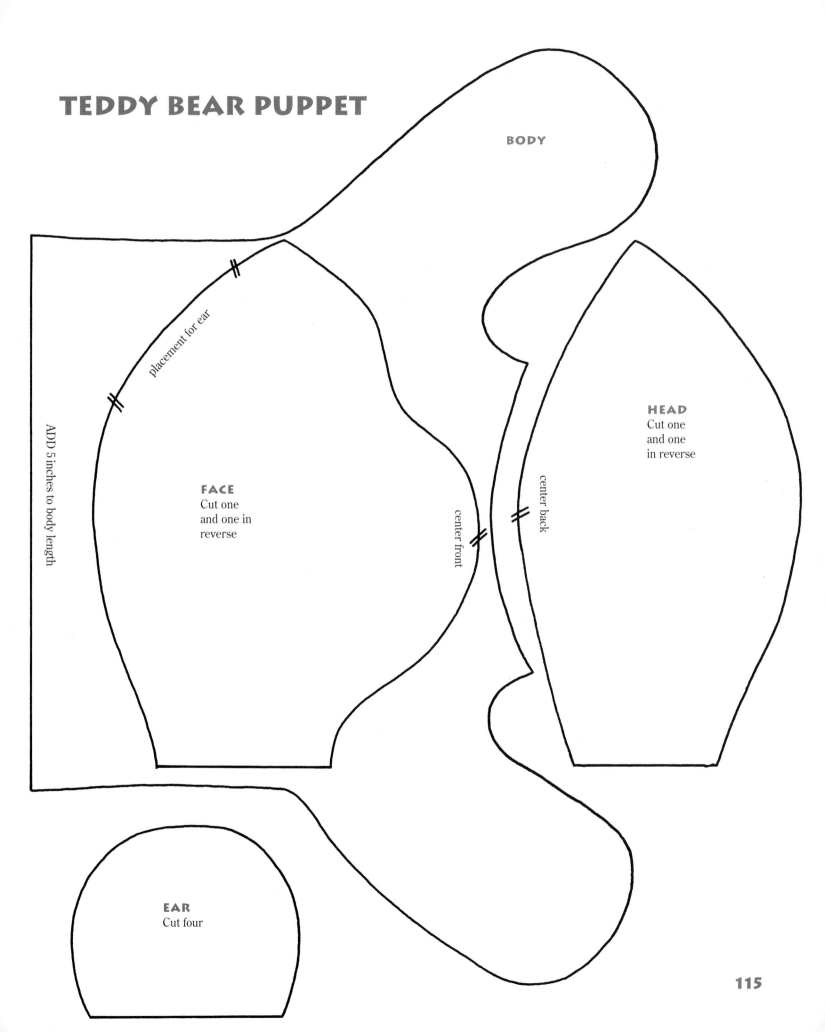

BODY

placement for ear

ADD 5 inches to body length

FACE
Cut one
and one in
reverse

center front

center back

HEAD
Cut one
and one
in reverse

EAR
Cut four

SASHIKO BAG

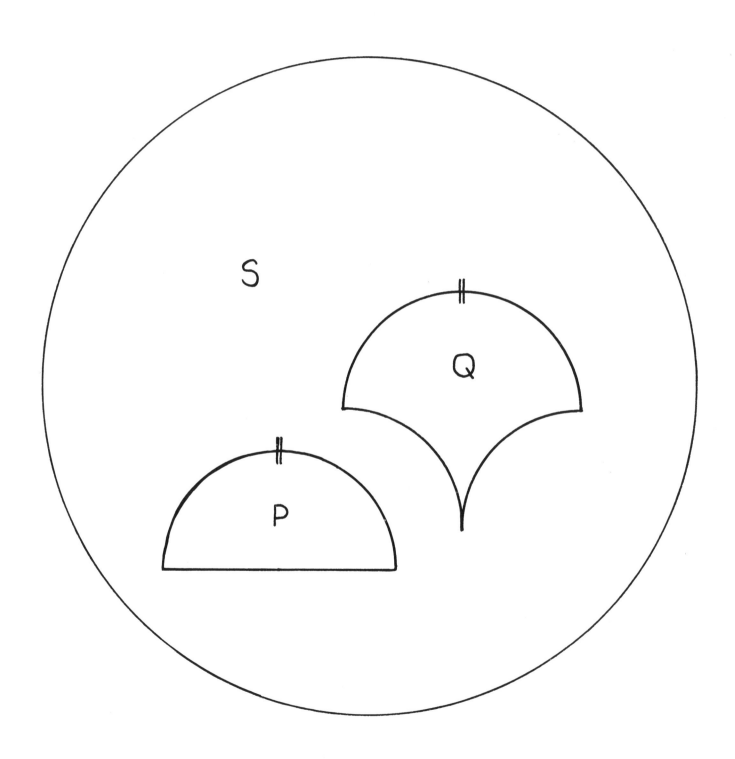

SUNFLOWER APRON

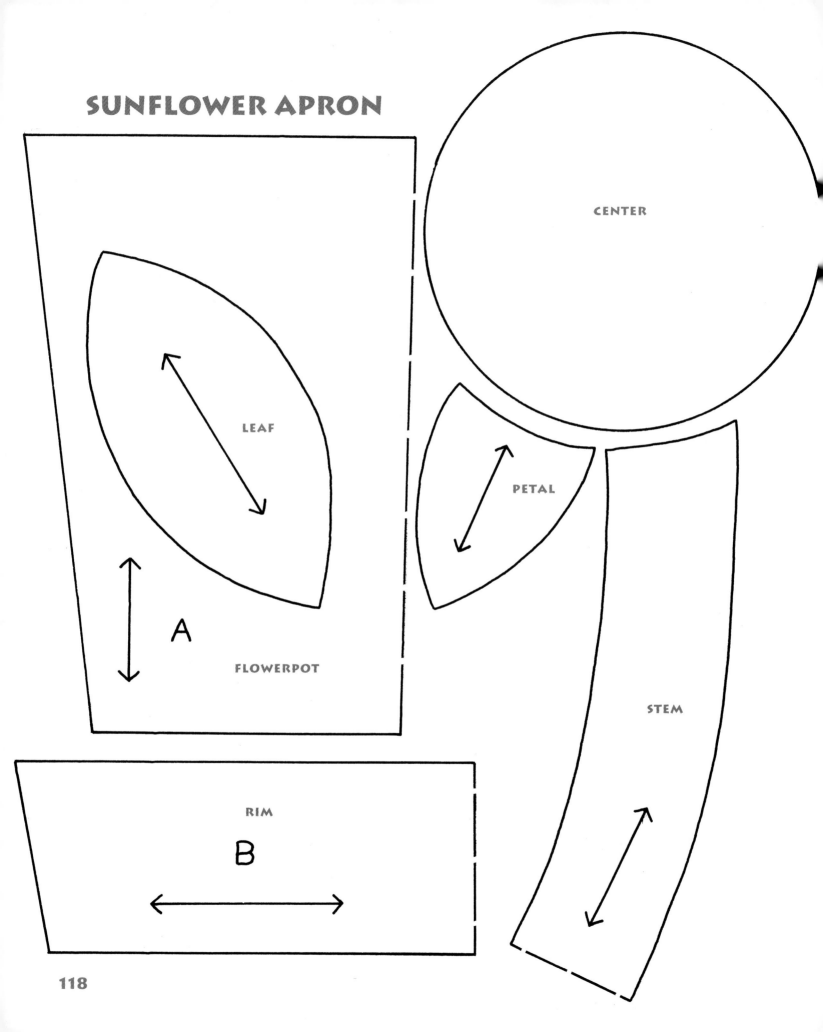

CENTER

LEAF

PETAL

A

FLOWERPOT

STEM

RIM

B

TEACUP APPLIQUÉ QUILT

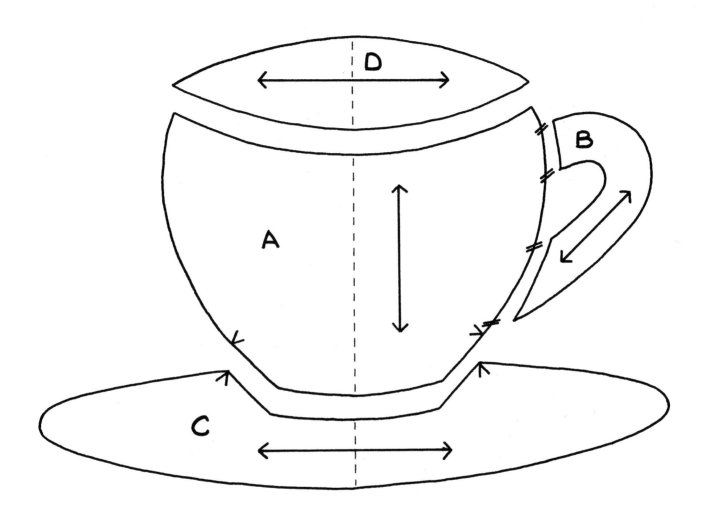

QUILTING PATTERNS
AMISH TABLE RUNNER

BASKET COT QUILT

TEACUP QUILT

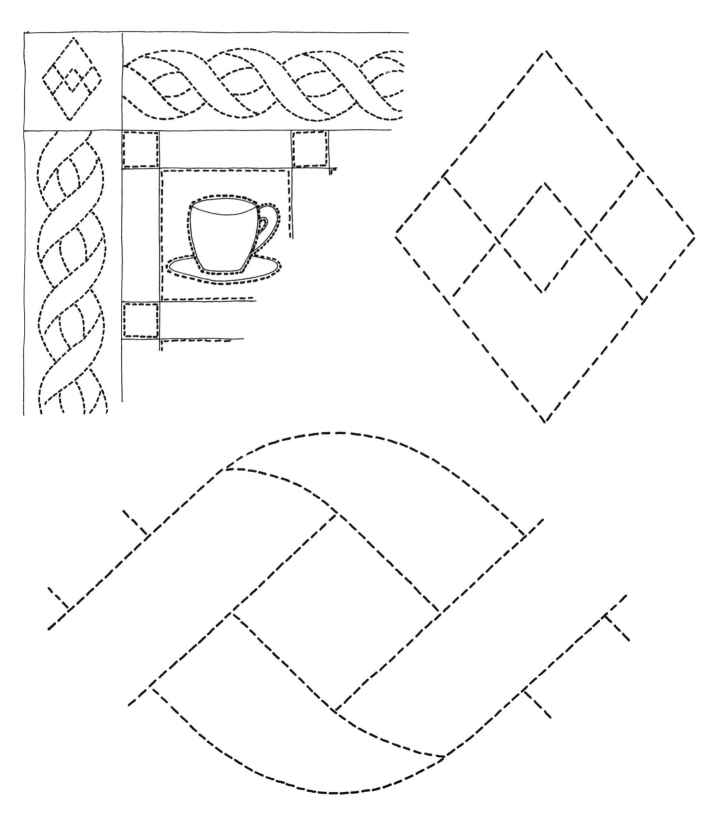

METRIC EQUIVALENCY CHART

INCHES TO MILLIMETRES AND CENTIMETRES

INCHES	MM	CM	INCHES	CM	INCHES	CM
1/8	3	0.3	9	22.9	30	76.2
1/4	6	0.6	10	25.4	31	78.7
3/8	10	1.0	11	27.9	32	81.3
1/2	13	1.3	12	30.5	33	83.8
5/8	16	1.6	13	33.0	34	86.4
3/4	19	1.9	14	35.6	35	88.9
7/8	22	2.2	15	38.1	36	91.4
1	25	2.5	16	40.6	37	94.0
1 1/4	32	3.2	17	43.2	38	96.5
1 1/2	38	3.8	18	45.7	39	99.1
1 3/4	44	4.4	19	48.3	40	101.6
2	51	5.1	20	50.8	41	104.1
2 1/2	64	6.4	21	53.3	42	106.7
3	76	7.6	22	55.9	43	109.2
3 1/2	89	8.9	23	58.4	44	111.8
4	102	10.2	24	61.0	45	114.3
4 1/2	114	11.4	25	63.5	46	116.8
5	127	12.7	26	66.0	47	119.4
6	152	15.2	27	68.6	48	121.9
7	178	17.8	28	71.1	49	124.5
8	203	20.3	29	73.7	50	127.0

YARDS TO METRES

YARDS	METRES	YARDS	METRES	YARDS	METRES	YARDS	METRES	YARDS	METRES
1/8	0.11	2 1/8	1.94	4 1/8	3.77	6 1/8	5.60	8 1/8	7.43
1/4	0.23	2 1/4	2.06	4 1/4	3.89	6 1/4	5.72	8 1/4	7.54
3/8	0.34	2 3/8	2.17	4 3/8	4.00	6 3/8	5.83	8 3/8	7.66
1/2	0.46	2 1/2	2.29	4 1/2	4.11	6 1/2	5.94	8 1/2	7.77
5/8	0.57	2 5/8	2.40	4 5/8	4.23	6 5/8	6.06	8 5/8	7.89
3/4	0.69	2 3/4	2.51	4 3/4	4.34	6 3/4	6.17	8 3/4	8.00
7/8	0.80	2 7/8	2.63	4 7/8	4.46	6 7/8	6.29	8 7/8	8.12
1	0.91	3	2.74	5	4.57	7	6.40	9	8.23
1 1/8	1.03	3 1/8	2.86	5 1/8	4.69	7 1/8	6.52	9 1/8	8.34
1 1/4	1.14	3 1/4	2.97	5 1/4	4.80	7 1/4	6.63	9 1/4	8.46
1 3/8	1.26	3 3/8	3.09	5 3/8	4.91	7 3/8	6.74	9 3/8	8.57
1 1/2	1.37	3 1/2	3.20	5 1/2	5.03	7 1/2	6.86	9 1/2	8.69
1 5/8	1.49	3 5/8	3.31	5 5/8	5.14	7 5/8	6.97	9 5/8	8.80
1 3/4	1.60	3 3/4	3.43	5 3/4	5.26	7 3/4	7.09	9 3/4	8.92
1 7/8	1.71	3 7/8	3.54	5 7/8	5.37	7 7/8	7.20	9 7/8	9.03
2	1.83	4	3.66	6	5.49	8	7.32	10	9.14

ACKNOWLEDGEMENTS

Writing this book has been the challenge of a lifetime and in the end, one of my most rewarding achievements. I could never have done it without the help, encouragement and support of my family, friends and colleagues.

I would like to especially thank my editor, Ljiljana Ortolja-Baird, for her cooperative spirit and patience in working hand in hand with a first time author; Susan and Gareth Jenkins for their vision and faith in me; the book's designers, Ed Harbour and Judy Gordon, whose gallant efforts behind the scenes helped make this book a reality; Carole Thomas, for her technical back-up; Maggie Wilkinson, for her administrative and all round support, and Penny Brown for her exquisite illustrations which bring the projects to life and give the book its unique appeal.

Many, many thanks to Adele Corcoran for her invaluable technical assistance, for helping me to make the Basket Quilt, Teacup Quilt, Sunflower Apron and Tic-Tac-Toe Game under very tight deadlines and for being available whenever I needed her regardless of the time. A special thank you to Pat Howarth for her outstanding workmanship in piecing and quilting the Amish Table Runner; Kazuko Takeguchi for her making of the Christmas Box and Sashiko Bag and her sister, Fumiko Ichikawa for the bag's inspired design; Di and Rob Wells, of *Patches* in Tewkesbury, for being so accommodating and helpful; Gul Laporte of *The Attic* and Maria-Zita for quilting the Teacup Quilt; *Quilter's Resource, USA* for the lamé used in the Tic-Tac-Toe project; and Brian Scales of the *Sewing Centre* in Battersea.

I would also like to express my appreciation to Dave Baird, Denis Corcoran, Tim Goodwin, Ray Gordon and Jill Connick who were very kind, understanding and supportive in taking up the slack caused by the frequent absence of their partners while this book was in the making.

On a more personal level, without the help of my nanny, Niamh Cusack, this book could not have been finished, regardless of the deadline. She exceeded all my expectations in managing my household and helping me care for my children with genuine kindness and love. A million apologies and thanks to my wonderful sons, Jeffrey and Tyler, for tolerating a preoccupied but always loving mum. Many thanks to my special friend and colleague, Linda Seward, who was always there with constructive criticism, creative ideas, moral support and the confidence that only years of writing quilt books can give. To my friends: Deb Mattsson, who lent me her sewing machine when mine expired under pressure, Gill Kelly, Barbara Clarke, Jenny Fitzherbert-Brockholes, Renate Mahmoud and Jennifer Stark-Portz who were always there for me and whose collective kindness, loyalty and friendship never failed. I am also grateful to Sally Goodyear, Maureen Dady, Ray and Katherine Daffurn, and Anny Evason and Hazel Smythe for their encouragement. A special thank you to Emily, Melissa, Jason, Carol and David Wilkin for sharing *Pinetum*, our home away from home, with me and my family.

Finally, I would like to thank my immediate family - Marcia, Jack, Mark, Hallie, and especially my husband Dave, whose love and subtle support gave me the confidence and encouragement I needed to persevere.